DARE TO SURVIVE

DARE TO SURVIVE

DEATH, HEARTBREAK, AND TRIUMPH IN THE WILD

RICK AND AMY RINEHART

FOREWORD BY BUTCH FARABEE

CITADEL PRESS
Kensington Publishing Corp.
www.Kensingtonbooks.com

CITADEL PRESS BOOKS are published by

Kensington Publishing Corp.
850 Third Avenue
New York, NY 10022

All Kensington titles, imprints, and distributed lines are available at special quantity discounts for bulk purchases for sales promotions, premiums, fund-raising, educational, or institutional use. Special book excerpts or customized printings can also be created to fit specific needs. For details, write or phone the office of the Kensington special sales manager: Kensington Publishing Corp., 850 Third Avenue, New York, NY 10022, attn: Special Sales Department; phone 1-800-221-2647.

CITADEL PRESS and the Citadel logo are Reg. U.S. Pat. & TM Off.

First printing: August 2008

10 9 8 7 6 5 4 3 2 1

Printed in the United States of America

Library of Congress Control Number: 2008922843

ISBN-13: 978-0-8065-2880-9
ISBN-10: 0-8065-2880-X

For our children—Kay, Brian, Alex, and CC

Be careful out there.

Contents

Foreword
by Butch Farabee

Nobody wants to die an ugly death, but it happens and more often than we know. People push their limits, travel life's margins, and/or stop thinking . . . but for a moment. *Dare to Survive* covers the full spectrum of mishap and mayhem, from avalanche to flashfloods, from plane wrecks to getting lost to being attacked by wild animals.

Reading *Dare to Survive* reminded me of some of the several thousand tragic and often bizarre events in which I was a player. Most of these were preventable and all certainly were needless. The cost in lifelong suffering alone is huge. All too many of these incidents, stored in some remote part of my brain, suddenly and graphically flashed back into my consciousness through the well-presented and sometimes almost voyeuristic episodes in this book.

I went on my first search at age sixteen in 1958 (all three Boy Scouts, one of whom was a classmate of mine, ended up dying of hypothermia while hiking) and then along the way spent three years on a large, metropolitan police department. Finally, I invested twenty-five of my thirty-four years with the National Park Service as a field ranger in several of our country's largest, most rugged, and highly visited national parks. I can personally testify to just how hard and miserable it is to spend hours and sometimes days in cold, wet, dark, windy, slippery, exposed, and dangerous circumstances while on a rescue, investigating an accident, diving in zero visibility, starting an IV on a cliff, and/or serving as a coroner in a body recovery.

When we saved a life it was an incredible emotional high—

thankfully for both us and more important, those we helped—this feeling of euphoria was often. Nothing is more exhilarating than jumping from a hovering helicopter into a river to snag an exhausted swimmer or to hear a faint "I'm here!" come out of the gloom when yelling into the night for a lost child. I remember these times with satisfaction and great clarity.

On the other hand, there were all-too-often times when my co-workers and I were not so lucky and were faced with assisting in a gruesome body recovery or untangling bloody people from a mangled car. Fortunately, these memories are blurring with time. Thankfully. Those tragedies always proved a source of great sorrow, especially when we knew the premature death was due to negligence, inattention, silly bravado, or inadequate knowledge or skill. By my estimate, I have been on 150 body recoveries and several times that many when someone's momentary failure of good sense or simple mistake resulted in something serious like lifelong paralysis or the loss of a major limb.

Dare to Survive brought back one mishap I remember the most—the singular freak accident that still brings tears to my eyes—the death of Colin Neu. The six-year-old was feeding potato chips to a young, spiked buck. His parents sat nearby, innocently oblivious of the danger. In but the blink it took for a startled deer to jerk its head up, the tiny boy now lay bleeding to death at their feet—gored accidentally by the wild animal. For ninety minutes, I performed CPR on the lad knowing, fearing I probably would not be successful. Colin's father sat prayerfully silent near me, watching as his son's life ebbed away before him. Hoping against hope, we twisted and bounced as the ambulance screamed off the mountain toward the surgical team waiting in Fresno. Was little Colin even old enough to have aspirations and dreams beyond his tomorrow? How did his parents deal with their grief? How much guilt do they still carry? Could we have done more to save this fragile child?

As all those who deal with life and death on a daily basis quickly learn, you cannot dwell on these events and the inevitable, second-guessing, gut-wrenching "only-ifs." But even so, you are never far removed from the sense of loss they seem always to spur. Regardless of how hardened first responders say they are, there is always the subtle shake of their collective heads and a quietly asked, "Why?"

Be prepared, however, because as the reader of *Dare to Survive*, you will get a large dose of this emotional-laden insight.

The pattern of accidents and incidents chronicled in *Dare to Survive* is very revealing and you should take note. This is serious business and there is much to learn here. Study the stories, and analyze the times and those conditions when people lived and when people died. Maybe you cannot prevent a similar accident, but maybe you can. Here are some thoughts on staying alive.

The first and most important thing is *do not panic!* The ultimate key to survive most of the incidents described in *Dare to Survive* is to keep your head. Assume full responsibility for your actions, emotions, and situations, and possess (or adopt) a positive mental attitude and powerful will to live.

If you hike, ski, climb, or go into the outdoors, *do not* go alone. *Always* tell someone where you are going. *Always* tell people when to expect your return. *Do not* totally rely on modern technology; cell phones and GPS units have value but are limited and will not replace common sense. *Always* and continually pay attention to where you are, where you have been, and where you are going. Situational awareness is critical; that is, know what is going on around you at all times. *Always* ask yourself, "what if." Prevention is far more preferable than the cure.

Nothing replaces intelligent prior planning and doing one's homework to avoid many of the situations found in this book. I hope you enjoy it. More important, however, I pray you will learn something from *Dare to Survive*.

Acknowledgments

The authors owe a debt of gratitude to Dave Jenney of Northland Press, who originally proposed the idea for this book and who sent us on a two-year adventure of vicarious exploration through newspapers, libraries, scientific journals, diaries, and of course the Internet. Though this book was ultimately published elsewhere, Dave is especially to be thanked for his graciousness and good humor during a particularly awkward time for all of us.

Many thanks to our agent Bob Diforio and our editor at Citadel, Michaela Hamilton, for their faith in us and this project.

Our good friend Carol Whitaker is to be thanked not only for sharing her diary of the 1998 manhunt in the Four Corners area with us, but also keeping us apprised of updates in the nearly ten-year-old case.

Tyler Wilcox is especially to be thanked for contributing much of the material in "Biblical Rains" and helping us make our publisher's deadline. (Well, almost.)

The following also granted permission to reprint certain material that appears in this book: Robert M. Timm, Director and Extension Wildlife Specialist, University of California Hopland Research and Extension Center, for data on coyote attacks in California; snowboarder Luke Edgar, for his account of surviving an avalanche; photographers Carol Whitaker and Annie Nelson; and artist Patrick Karnahan for his depiction of the last flight of "123."

Search and rescue icon and National Park Service honoree for "exemplifying the best of the ranger tradition," Charles R. "Butch" Farabee graciously agreed to write the foreword and permitted us to excerpt passages from his book *Death, Daring, and Disaster: Search and Rescue in the National Parks.*

Finally, the authors would like to thank the late George H. D. Rinehart for reviewing several chapters and bringing fifty years of editing experience to bear on this book. We'd like to think that his spirit lives on under the western sky he so loved, strumming his Gibson somewhere and belting out a Woody Guthrie ballad to an audience of coyotes and rabbitbrush.

DARE TO SURVIVE

Introduction

Perhaps science will one day ultimately be found to be at the heart of religion, or faith . . . but for now, no such explanation or discovery exists, only the inexplicable awareness that there is a difference between the West and the rest of the country, and that it is no less profound for its ungraspable immeasurability.

—Rick Bass

It was late November high in the Klamath Mountains of southwestern Oregon and the family of four was hopelessly lost in the snow. They had been attempting to cross the mountains to reach the Oregon coast and its gentler climate, but the normally reliable sense of direction of the parents, Jim and Kati, had eluded them. Stranded with their two small daughters, Penelope—four, and Sabine—seven months, the family subsisted on berries and crackers for a time and burned what dry wood they could find to keep warm. When food ran out, Kati breast-fed both girls. Finally, on the ninth day of their ordeal, Jim decided their only hope was for him to hike out and try to find some semblance of civilization in the vast wilderness. He promised to return if he failed to make contact with anyone. When Jim didn't return after two days, Kati took the two girls and started walking down the only road in the vicinity. Remarkably, they were able to find help within hours.

Searchers then went to look for Jim, following footprints in the snow as well as a trail of clothes he had deliberately discarded to either lead a possible rescuer to him or to help him find his way back to his family. On Wednesday, December 6, his body was found facedown in a creek whose icy water was one to two feet deep. Trackers noted that he had walked five miles west of where he had left his family, circled back to within a half mile of them, then succumbed to hypothermia. In a heroic effort to save his family in country described as "snowy terrain with sodden branches, slick rocks, downed trees, and poison oak," he had frozen to death.

What resonates as a tale of heroism from the nineteenth-century American frontier actually occurred in late November and early December 2006, when the Kim family of San Francisco, California, exited off Interstate 5 to take what they thought was a back road to Gold Beach, Oregon. After encountering heavy snow on Bear Camp Road, they detoured onto a logging road on Bureau of Land Management land near the Wild Rogue Wilderness. Unbeknown to the Kims, the road should have been closed, but BLM officials had kept it open, believing there were still hunters in the area who needed to get out. After a few hours, the Kims found themselves hopelessly snowbound.

The Kims's story informs the premise of this book, which is that notwithstanding two centuries of human development, exploitation, and extraction, the American West remains a place where nature must be respected, especially when it manifests itself in extremes of weather, climate, geography, and topography found in few other places on Earth. Moreover, the conveniences and comforts of life in the twenty-first century have not always come to our rescue in confronting these elements, especially when we deliberately leave them behind to explore those parts of the West that are still barren of human habitation—still wild.

That we are generally city dwellers makes it easy to forget one fundamental truth about our continent: there's still a lot of vacant land out there. Indeed, as of 2001, only 5.5 percent of the total land area of the contiguous forty-eight states was classified as "developed land" by the U.S. Department of Agriculture, a figure undoubtedly skewed by, as one writer has put it, the West's "miles and miles of miles and miles." Seventy-two percent of all developed land is classified as "urban," while 20 percent is said to be used for "rural transportation." (Presumably this would mean highway and railroad easements.) For all our talk of urban sprawl and congestion, outside of agriculture our presence on the land is really quite small. Although no one would ever want to try it, the 37 million residents of California could all lie down and take a nap together in an area roughly the size of Los Angeles International Airport—and still leave enough room to land a 747 or two.

Nevertheless, the fact that so much land remains "undeveloped" does not imply that humans have not had a role in its management—far from it, in fact. Roughly 60 percent of all undeveloped land is used as cropland or range and pasture land; forestry and mining occur on both vast public and private lands. Of course, a lot of land is dedicated to recreation and preservation, some is classified as wilderness, and very little of it that isn't already physically inaccessible is deemed to be strictly off limits.

But just because we are using the land in various ways does not make it any less wild, dangerous, or unforgiving of human folly. Indeed, this book has been written with the firm belief that the adjective "natural" does not in any way imply the absence of human beings. Over the years there has been arrogance on all sides of this issue, but none more so than those who deign to know the true definition of nature as if it was as clearly delineated as a national park boundary. In a broad sense, we are all a part of nature in an ever-evolving global ecosystem. Although an excess of anything is not always a good thing, Americans for the most part have done a remarkably good job of balancing economic exigency with prudent land use. Notorious exceptions to this abound, of course—one need only recall the systematic extermination of predators in the past century to make the point—but we must also recognize that our views toward and knowledge of the natural world have matured.

Moreover, they have matured because our prosperity has allowed them to. Wolves would never have been reintroduced into Yellowstone without the willingness of well-funded conservation organizations to compensate ranchers for livestock losses due to wolf predation. Wilderness areas would not have been set aside if circumstances were so desperate that the lands were needed for mining or logging. True, battles are fought every day over the preservation of wild lands, but these are relatively minor skirmishes that in their totality do not a larger conflict make. It's been a long time since any national debate has taken place over flooding a canyon for hydro-electric power or creating a new national park. The controversy over drilling in the Alaska National Wildlife Refuge comes close, but even with our dependence on foreign oil we seem to be able to afford the luxury of tabling the issue after the token congressional consideration. All of which reinforces what should be a society's primary goal in formulating sound environmental policy: make it wealthy.

Locally, of course, land use is an ongoing give-and-take rife with unintended consequences and inevitable compromises. The good news is that we have a great deal of control over what happens locally because it is quite simply in our immediate self-interest to make our surroundings pleasant, safe, and interesting to us. Air pollution in places like Denver and Los Angeles has been reduced substantially over the past twenty years because residents demanded cleaner air. Citizens in certain western communities have agreed to be taxed to purchase large greenbelts or buffer zones to keep communities away from one another. And to some extent open space ecosystems have been restored or enhanced to allow us to live side by side with a reasonable construct of the pre-settlement West. As long as we have the space and can afford it, it seems, we will try to take advantage of what photographer Robert Adams once referred to as "a western scale that, despite our crowding, persists in long views."

How far we go in accommodating nature of the nonhuman kind, though, remains to be seen. Twenty years ago the sighting of a bear or cougar near our communities would have been a rare and wondrous thing. Though today wildlife incursions have almost become a nuisance, we are ambivalent about how to deal with them. As is fully discussed early in this book, the surprising response to a wild animal attack is that there often is no response—no public outcry, no call for revenge against the animal (especially if it's a bear or cougar). Perhaps it is the Westerner's view that a little wildness comes with the territory.

These changes and others on a broader scale have left the modern environmental movement in a confused state. Forty years ago, the agenda was lengthy and enjoyed wide public support: set aside more land for preservation; reintroduce wildlife where it had been exterminated; reduce air and water pollution; control human impact on public lands; and increase appreciation for biological and ecological processes. Although much work needs to be done and as stewards of the land we can't let down our vigilance, that so much has been achieved has led to the green activist's version of empty nest syndrome. With so many environmental issues becoming mainstream on both sides of the American political divide, the only way for many of today's environmental activists to regain their former clout is to lay the explanation for every natural calamity at the hand of man and create a nongovernmental organization to attract contributions and lobby politicians.

Though we are agnostic on the issue of whether or not humans have contributed to climate change, it is clear that some activists have overplayed their hands on the matter. One of the purposes of this book is to respond to the conceit that humans actually have all that much control over nature. Can we really set the global temperature by adding or subtracting carbon dioxide? Can we define what "optimal" weather is to prevent killer blizzards, flash floods, and tornadoes? While we can affect change for the better or worse on a modest scale in global terms, what we broadly refer to as the forces of nature still hold the ultimate trump card over all of humanity.

To reinforce this view, we limited our research into these tales of peril in the face of nature to events that occurred within the past twenty-five years, a period whose exponential growth in communication and digital technology couldn't overcome the mishaps that befell the victims. The accounts were selected for their human interest and ability to serve as cautionary tales for what *not* to do while outdoors in the American West, which for the purposes of this book is defined as the lands west of the Mississippi, excluding Alaska and Hawaii. They are meant to be neither comprehensive nor complete; they are, however, meant to be informative and at times entertaining. The theme of each chapter has been informed by the quality and quantity of the material available to us, and we have attempted to place events in the larger picture by providing an overview of such natural phenomena as western weather and climate, wildlife migrations, geography, topography, and forest succession. The conclusion, Two Weeks in September, is a snapshot of fourteen days in September 2007 that came to crystallize many of the topics presented in this book.

Underlying the accounts that follow is our abiding respect for, and love of, the western landscape and the good people who have been its stewards. Living ninety minutes from the Wyoming border in urban Colorado, one of our favorite pastimes is to slip the noose of the Boulder–Denver metropolitan area and lose ourselves in the Cowboy State and beyond for a few days. With nothing but two-lane blacktop beneath you and no prospect of a rest area for a hundred miles, even a mild sense of vulnerability can be exhilarating, and miles of unfettered landscape can provide a lot of perspective for a comparatively insignificant human being. In such moments we recall the famous words of a young woman who lost her life in the Teton Mountains long ago: "God bless Wyoming and keep it wild."

I

THEIRS IS THE KINGDOM: ANIMAL ATTACKS

Of all the enduring symbols of the American West, perhaps none is greater than that of some large mammal—wapiti, moose, or grizzly bear—nobly cresting a ridgeline surrounded by unfettered wilderness. Romantic though this image may be, the fact is that the plains and mountains west of the Mississippi support a remarkable number of wild animals whose populations have been in flux since the first white human settlement appeared two hundred years ago. And they have lived in what can only be described as an uneasy compatibility among their hominid neighbors, keeping to themselves in protected habitat of one kind or another. Only when the boundaries of habitat and human civilization overlap or become otherwise obfuscated does the possibility for danger to both man and animal increase. Just as nothing good seldom happens in a bar after 1 a.m., something bad will inevitably happen to a careless photographer who gets between a grizzly bear sow and her cubs. And it has.

The Yellowstone ecosystem, the area that comprises Yellowstone and Grant Teton national parks and surrounding public lands, has been called the "Serengeti of North America" for all the large mammals that inhabit the area, but this shortchanges even vaster tracts of undeveloped land in the West that are home to huge populations of ungulates, or hoofed mammals. Pronghorn in Wyoming, for example, probably outnumber the human population, which a recent census put at about 515,000 souls. Although the elk population in Yellowstone has fallen by half in recent years due to wolf predation and persistent drought, the overall western population is stable at about 750,000 animals. (Indeed, another national park, Rocky Mountain, has about twice the number of elk—3,000—that is considered sustainable. Officials are now considering allowing hunters into the park to "cull" the herds.) Though no reliable estimate is available, the population of mule, whitetail, and black tail deer in the West probably numbers over 10 million. All of these figures reflect a robust recovery from mid-twentieth-century populations decimated by hunting and habitat loss.

The animals that we perceive as dangerous for their ferocity—bears, lions, and canines—are also making a substantial comeback, to the point of making bold incursions into our streets and neighborhoods. The low end for black bear numbers in the West (excluding Alaska) is more than 100,000; for grizzlies the number is a comparatively low 1,200, but this is up substantially from when the bear was first listed as a "threatened" species by the U.S. Fish and Wildlife Service in 1975. (Calling its recovery "remarkable" and "an amazing accomplishment," Deputy Interior Secretary Lynn Scarlett announced on March 22, 2007, that the grizzly no longer needed protection of the Endangered Species Act.) Though mountain lions (also known as pumas, panthers, painters, deer tigers, catamounts, and just plain lions) once ranged the entire continent, today their stronghold is primarily the western United States and Canada, where they are in sufficient numbers to warrant being listed as a game animal in most states. Wolves also once roamed the entire United States and Canada, but were nearly exterminated in the western United States by the 1930s. Fortunately, attitudes toward this magnificent predator changed by the late twentieth century, and a successful reintroduction program brought the gray wolf back to northern Montana, Idaho, and Yellowstone National Park in the late 1990s. Still, wolf numbers in the American West are quite low, with some 650 animals found in the northern Rockies, and a southern variant, the Mexican Gray Wolf, numbering perhaps a hundred in Arizona and New Mexico. The wolf's wily cousin, the coyote, has proved far more adaptable to habitat change, and has even increased its range well beyond western borders; one was even captured in New York's Central Park in 2006. Because of its elusiveness, firm numbers are hard to come by and estimates of the coyote population for the entire United States can range from 1 million to 10 million animals.

But it has been the growing human population of the American West that has led to the increase in dangerous encounters with wild animals and not the other way around. As many threatened, endangered, or just plain diminished animal species have started to recover to their pre-settlement numbers (or so we think), the human population in sixteen western states averaged an aggregate growth rate of 8.8 percent from 2000 to 2006 alone, with Nevada at the high end (24.9 percent) and South Dakota at the low end (4.3 percent). Growth restriction ordinances in some cities have ironically contributed to the problem, pushing development onto land not already designated for open space or habitat preservation and inadvertently interfering with wildlife corridors. Indeed, identifying and in some cases creating wildlife corridors seems to have become the latest challenge to scientists as some large mammal populations have recovered. Still, a pedestrian greenway constructed in a riparian corridor only becomes a corridor for *both* wildlife and humans, leading to encounters that can be as innocuous as a bird-watching experience or as deadly as a cougar attack.

Naturally, an attack by a large wild animal is going to get more attention than a bee sting (which can be equally dangerous to some), but this reinforces our fascination with the wild and the beasts that constitute its romantic symbols. Though the mosquito is probably the deadliest animal on Earth by virtue of its capacity to spread disease, there's nothing like an elephant stampede or a tiger mauling (however rare) to give rise to "the wolf in the heart," as Theodore Roosevelt once proclaimed about the wild. An attack by a large mammal is still a frightening and occasionally tragic event, and the fact that they are happening with increasing frequency in the American West is cause for concern, if not quite yet a cause for alarm. Much can be done to avoid an attack, and a deeper understanding of a wild animal's natural history and behavior is the best place to start. Unfortunately, even this knowledge hasn't been enough to save some people from a fatal rendezvous with a man-eater.

Cute, Endearing, and Occasionally Deadly: The Black Bear

North America is home to approximately 750,000 black bears living in a variety of habitats, making it perhaps one of the continent's most adaptable large mammals. Sixteen subspecies can be found in such diverse locales as the Florida Everglades, New England, the Kenai Peninsula of Alaska, northeastern Mexico, and of course the American West and Southwest. Black bears are not always black; in the Rocky Mountains nearly half may be brown or "cinnamon," and some may actually appear blond. (A rare white species, *Ursus americanus kermodei*, inhabits coastal British Columbia.)

Black bears differ from grizzly bears in many significant ways. At four to seven feet in length, black bears are smaller than grizzly bears (indeed, black bears are the smallest of all North American bear species); males can weigh from 125 to 500 pounds, females between 90 and 300 pounds. Black bears also reproduce more quickly than grizzly bears; sows can have up to six litters of two cubs during their lifetimes. Black bears climb trees; grizzlies do not. Though grizzly bears are omnivores, eating everything from fish, to elk, to insects, about 75 percent of the black bear's diet is vegetarian. In times of drought a black bear will range well beyond its home territory in search of food, often found in the lush landscaped backyards or trash bins of suburbanites. (In fact, human garbage is popular with both grizzly and black bears because it provides a quick way to add on calories prior to denning. Yellowstone officials regularly permitted bears to eat from the park's garbage dumps until the mid-1970s.) Black bears are opportunistic carnivores and, being generally too slow to catch small animals, will feed on fish, carrion, and newborn or small ungulates to enhance their largely vegetarian diet.

Expectedly, black bears tend to show aggression when competing for food or a mate, but tend to bluff more than actually attack. Observers of bear behavior suggest that a bear may make "threats" by first sniffing the air, followed by looking directly at the threatened individual, then charging or feinting a charge—and perhaps suddenly stopping to pound the ground and "huff" for effect—and then either stand, or simply walk or run away.

Though tolerance reflects the black bear's normal disposition toward human beings, the University of Calgary biologist Stephen Herrero, in his landmark study *Bear Attacks: Their Causes and Avoidance*, reminds us that black bears can "bite through live trees thicker than a man's arm. They can kill a full-grown steer with a bite to the neck." Still, Herrero concludes, "Rarely . . . do black bears use their power to injure or kill people . . . most . . . can become accustomed to people and their foods without endangering human lives." The numbers would appear to support this view. Herrero has cited twenty-three records of people killed by black bears in all of North

The ubiquitous black bear. (National Park Service, Yellowstone National Park)

America from 1900 to 1980. Another less verifiable source has put the number at fifty-two from 1900 to 2007, only three of which are said to have occurred in the American West.

Still, black bear encounters have become increasingly common in the early twenty-first century. The summer of 2006 produced an unusually high number of bear sightings and/or incidents, including one that interrupted a triathlon for one cyclist outside of Boulder, Colorado. As reported in the *Denver Post*:

> Triathlete Sabrina Oei was speeding downhill at nearly 40 mph, cycling through the Colorado foothills during a race, when something brought her to a sudden, painful, stop: a bear.

The bear had wandered onto the race course and directly into Oei's path, the ensuing collision sending the cyclist airborne. After a painful landing on the pavement, Oei managed to pull herself together and finish the triathlon. By all accounts the bear seemed to have recovered as well and was last seen escaping back into the woods.

The *Post* also cited five other incidents that had already occurred that spring and summer. On July 2 in Lake Tahoe a bear had made himself comfortable in a parked convertible and gorged on pizza and beer in full view of a small crowd. On June 26 wildlife officials had to tranquilize a bear that had taken up residence in the backyard of a Santa Fe homeowner. Bear sightings were so common in a city park in Ashland, Oregon, that officials had to post warnings during the city's famous outdoor Shakespeare festival in May. Utah wildlife officers had to kill a bear that had attacked a Boy Scout a mere forty miles from Salt Lake City. And one bear even dared crossing Interstate 25 near Cheyenne on June 13. Although it posed no threat to humans, it probably posed a threat to itself in its meanderings; officials captured and later relocated it to the nearby mountains from where it had presumably come.

The increasing frequency of incidents was bound to produce a fatality, and one occurred on the night of June 27, 2007, when an eleven-year-old boy was dragged by a black bear from the tent he was sharing with his family in Utah's American Fork Canyon. His body was later discovered about four hundred yards from the tent. The attack tragically underscored Herrero's conclusion that predation was most likely the motive in the fatal incidents he had studied, and that half of the victims were children. The Utah incident followed more than a dozen black bear sightings in the region during the previous three weeks. State wildlife hunters, who had unsuccessfully tried to track the troublesome bear prior to the fatal mauling, used twenty-six search hounds and a helicopter to ultimately corner the bear in American Fork Canyon, where it was shot at 11:40 a.m. the following Monday. Prior to the Utah occurrence, the most recent fatality had taken place in Colorado on August 10, 1993, when a 240-pound black bear broke into a trailer and crushed the skull of twenty-four-year-old Colin McLelland.

Approximately five hundred black bear attacks have been reported in our state and national parks alone over the past ninety years or so, proving that the odds of surviving such an attack are actually quite high. And unlike the response to an attacking grizzly bear, the best way to avoid serious injury from a black bear might just be to fight back. As Stephen Herrero writes in *Bear Attacks*, "One need not be a prizefighter to deter a black bear." Black bears can be intimidated, even by just waving a stick or throwing a rock. (In the summer of 2007 an ex-Marine camping with his two sons in Georgia managed to kill an attacking bear by hitting it in the head with a log.) If a black bear is attacking to get at your food, however, the best course of action may be to give the food to the bear. And because black bears sometimes attack when feeling closed in on, merely giving it some space by backing off can deter an attack. (However, it is important to note that black bears, unlike grizzlies, are not likely to attack people in defense of cubs.) If the bear's motive is clearly predation, though—that is, it wants to kill you and eat you—Herrero suggests three possible outcomes: "The attack typically continues until the bear is forced to back down, or the person gets away, or the bear gets its prey. People who run away, unless they have somewhere to go, or people who act passively or play dead, are simply inviting the bear to continue the attack."

For all the talk and fear about what black bears can do to us, it's worth remembering that humans are the black bear's single biggest predator, both intentionally and unintentionally. Many states classify the black bear as a game animal, and the website for the North American Bear Center in Ely, Minnesota, states, "Very few bears outside of national parks die of natural causes. Nearly all adult bears die from human-related causes. Most are eventually shot. A few are killed by vehicles."

The American King of Beasts:
The Grizzly Bear

No single accomplishment in the past fifty years has better symbolized the return of the American West to some of its pre-settlement wildness than the recovery of the grizzly bear in Yellowstone National Park, and in parts of Montana, Idaho, Wyoming, and Washington. (There is speculation that remnant grizzlies inhabit the San Juan Mountains of Colorado, but the last verifiable sighting there was in 1979.) Though grizzlies once roamed the entire continental United States, incompatibility with human settlement quickly became apparent as the nation expanded, and the bear was hunted to near extinction for its depredations on domestic livestock, and yes, humans. (And lest there be any illusions about Native Americans living in harmony with the grizzly bear, one report from New York in 1814 quoted the Mohicans as having complained of a grizzly "very destructive to their nation, killing and devouring them." They ultimately killed the bear "after great difficulty.") Scientists estimate that the bear was eliminated from 98 percent of its original range in the lower forty-eight during a hundred-year period, surviving only in large and remote wilderness areas.

Unlike the black bear, a grizzly needs a lot of room to subsist successfully, which explains why sparsely populated Alaska has always been able to support a healthy population of grizzlies. Scientists have determined that grizzly populations in the northern Rockies in 1920 only survived to the present because they occupied areas larger than about 10,500 square miles. Individual bears may have

17

ranges up to 1,250 square miles, depending on food availability. As Paul Schullery has pointed out in his classic overview of Yellowstone's bears, "It is important that bear needs are not confused with human ambition for territory." Logically, Schullery explains, bears with large ranges are having the hardest time finding nutritious food, animal or vegetable. Their meanderings also put them at the increasing risk of encountering enemies or stumbling into accidents. Bears with small ranges, however, have the best chance to survive because they're probably finding everything they need nearby.

Grizzly bears differ from black bears physically with their pronounced shoulder hump, dish-shaped face, and of course larger size. Females can weigh anywhere from 250 to 750 pounds, males 350 to 1,150 pounds. The average female is about five feet in length from nose to tail, with males averaging nearly a foot longer. Grizzlies are commonly brown (which is why they are also called brown bears), but also can be blond or black or some combination of all three colors. Another physical characteristic that distinguishes grizzlies from black bears are their long, curved claws, which they use for everything from taking apart a log full of insects to excavating dens. One trait common to both grizzlies and black bears, though, is their elusive speed and quickness: both bears can reach 25 miles

Grizzly sow with cubs. You never want to be as close as this. (National Park Service, Yellowstone National Park)

per hour in a flat run. However, notwithstanding the grizzly bear's tremendous strength and impressive claws, it is not a tree climber except in rare circumstances.

Grizzly bears are opportunistic omnivores, taking advantage of what nature has available for them from spring through fall. Favored foods include white bark pine nuts, roots, berries, and even moths. (If you're picturing a grizzly swatting moths out of the air, let us dispel you of that image. In summer, cutworm moths in Yellowstone tend to load up on nectar in the morning, then gather on nearby rocks for the rest of the day. Grizzlies eat them in abundance, downing some 10,000 to 20,000 moths in a day.) The grizzly's diet is largely carnivorous when it first emerges from its den in the spring, when vegetation is scarce. As Schullery points out, because the bears are physically depleted from hibernation and can't range very far in search of food, carrion from winter kill is usually the most convenient source of nutrition. Grizzlies have even been known to excavate their dens close to known spring carcass concentrations. Grizzlies of course also feed on vulnerable living animals, such as newborn elk, sheep, and deer, as well as small rodents.

Grizzlies are generally not predisposed to attack humans on sight; the most common reaction is for the bear to simply flee. Like the black bear, grizzlies will often bluff an attack and charge to within a few feet of a person before running away. However, there are myriad reasons for a grizzly to attack where a black bear wouldn't, among them defending cubs, habituation to human scents and waste (i.e. garbage), provocation (especially by photographers!), and difficulty with normal feeding due to old age. Although fatal attacks on humans are quite rare, grizzlies attack with more frequency than black bears judging by the numbers. During the same period (1900–2007) that black bears killed three people in the western United States, grizzlies attacked and killed thirteen. (Keep in mind that black bear populations in the West have probably averaged more than 100,000 bears to the grizzly's 1,000 or less.) Moreover, out of some 165 recorded grizzly attacks for all of North America, almost 30 pecent have proved fatal.

The 1980s saw a rash of fatal grizzly bear attacks in the two large national parks that sustain them, Yellowstone and Glacier. The decade began with two deaths in Glacier National Park in late July 1980, and we know more detail about these cases than we normally would because *Bear Attacks* author Stephen Herrero served on the board of inquiry at the request of Glacier superintendent Phillip Iverson. The two victims, Jane Ammerman, female, and Kim Eberly, male, had been camping illegally in the park between a small resort area under development and an established campground. More important, their campsite was a half mile from a small garbage dump on a private inholding surrounded by the Blackfoot Indian reservation. Glacier had long since closed all of its dumps because of bear issues, and indeed had encouraged the owners of the private dump to shut it down as well. Making matters worse, Herrero's team found a decaying horse carcass in the dump, whose putrid aroma was capable of attracting bears from miles away. Herrero surmised that the bear that killed Ammerman and Eberly was probably traveling to or from the dump when after midnight on July 24 it came across the teenagers' campsite. Unusual for Glacier, the night was hot and muggy, prompting the couple to sleep on, rather than in, their tent. The bear might also have been attracted to body odor from sexual intercourse, but this, as Herrero is quick to add, is "conjecture."

The partially consumed bodies of the couple were found the next day, and members of the Blackfoot Tribe shot a grizzly bear nearby. The grizzly's dentition matched that of the bite marks on the dead campers' bodies. Furthermore, scat collected at the site of the killing indicated that the bear had been feeding on garbage just prior to the incident.

The following September another camper, Lawrence Gordon, was killed at the Elizabeth Lake campsite in Glacier's Belly River valley. Once again, the culprit was a bear habituated to humans, but not necessarily because of access to human food or garbage. It may have just gotten accustomed to having people around. Its foray into Gordon's camp and subsequent attack was probably a combination of "its past experience with people and a new urge," according to Herrero.

A fatal bear attack in Yellowstone in late July 1984 was particularly insidious because the victim had done nearly everything right to avoid it. Brigitta Fredenhagen of Basel, Switzerland, appeared to be a capable camper when she presented herself to park ranger Gary Youngblood on July 29 to take out a back-country hiking permit.

However, Youngblood did warn her about the area where she was headed, just north of a location favored by bears. Perhaps this is why she camped at White Lake, a few miles short of the site she had gotten the camping permit for. When Fredenhagen didn't show up at a prearranged meeting place and time with her brother and his wife the following day, Andreas Fredenhagen contacted park officials, who sent out three rangers on the morning of August 1 in search of her.

A ranger on horseback came across Fredenhagen's campsite at approximately 11 a.m. What he found would have shocked even the most battle-hardened corpsman: a torn dome tent; her sleeping bag, some six feet away, next to which were pieces of lip and scalp; and then her body some 250 feet away—much of which had been eaten.

A subsequent inquiry stressed that Fredenhagen had taken all the necessary precautions to avoid such an attack. It appears that she had eaten precooked or cold food and had only boiled water for tea. She had cached her food ninety feet from the camp in a rucksack hung up between two trees. The items in her tent were neatly arranged and her cleanliness was said to be outstanding. She had even made a note in her diary that she had followed all of the safeguards recommended by Youngblood at the time she secured the permit.

So what happened? Park officials inferred from the evidence that Fredenhagen had been pulled from the tent by her head and neck sometime after 10:30 p.m. on July 29. The bear in all likelihood was a young grizzly, because the food cache had been torn out of the trees and signs indicated that a bear had climbed twelve feet up one of the trees to get at it. (Sub-adult bears are more likely to climb trees than adult bears.) Fredenhagen had also unknowingly camped in an area that featured both hiking and game trails, and grizzlies are known to use both while traveling at night. Fredenhagen's one mistake, if it can be called that, may have been the decision to camp alone. After speaking with park biologists, Herrero opined in *Bear Attacks* that "prior conditions that allowed a grizzly bear to become used to people" may have contributed to the attack. The bear was never found.

The most recent fatal grizzly attack (outside of Canada and Alaska, of course) occurred in 1998 in Glacier National Park, and was a classic example of a grizzly sow coming to the defense of her cubs. On May 17, Glacier Park Company employee Craig Dahl apparently stumbled across the bear and her two cubs while hiking along Scenic Point Trail. His remains were discovered three days later, but so little was left of him that park officials had to call in the Glacier County sheriff/coroner Gary Racine to confirm they were Dahl's. "All that was left of his body was a few bigger bones, skull, and a small piece of skin," recalled Racine. Two hiking boots nearby contained Dahl's feet. Still, it took an analysis of bear scat found at the scene to confirm that grizzlies had in all probability killed Dahl. Tests confirmed that the scat contained human DNA.

DNA also confirmed the identity of the sow grizzly, a thirteen-year-old bear known as Chocolate Legs. The bear and her brood had been identified in a campground just outside of the park the year before and were then considered a mild nuisance. After the Dahl killing, however, park officials tracked her down and shot her. One of her cubs was also captured but kept alive for a time in an attempt to attract its twin. This failed, and four days later the captured cub was euthanized. (A colorful and speculative reconstruction of the attack on Dahl can be found in Roland Cheek's *Chocolate Legs: Sweet Mother, Savage Killer?* published by Skyline Publishing, Columbia Falls, Montana.)

Of course, not all grizzly attacks are fatal, and survival stories can be instructive in telling us how to avoid serious injury or death. In September 2005, for example, a physical therapist and his eighteen-year-old daughter were attacked by a grizzly bear in Glacier National Park trying to protect its cubs. The girl, Jenna Otter, suffered a bite on her heel and some cuts on her face before her father successfully diverted the bear's attention to him. The bear bit Johan Otter's thigh and clawed his face as Johan attempted, in vain, to strangle the bear. Tumbling onto the ground, Otter assumed the fetal position, covering his head with his arms. Though the bear still managed to bite a part of Otter's scalp that remained exposed, that was the end of the struggle, and the bear wandered off. In the five-minute attack, Otter had fractured five vertebrae, broken three ribs, fractured an eye socket, and received five major bites, but the fact that he had quickly assumed the fetal position probably saved his life.

Curling up in the fetal position is just one of several recommendations provided by the National Park Service for hikers who surprise bears in the backcountry. Others include:

✔ Talk quietly or not at all; the time to make loud noise is before you encounter a bear. Try to detour around the bear if possible.

✔ Do not run! Back away slowly, but stop if it seems to agitate the bear.

✔ Assume a nonthreatening posture. Turn sideways, or bend at the knees to appear smaller.

✔ Use peripheral vision. Bears appear to interpret direct eye contact as threatening.

✔ Drop something (not food) to distract the bear. Keep your pack on for protection in case of an attack.

✔ If a bear attacks and you have bear spray, use it!

✔ If the bear makes contact, protect your chest and abdomen by falling to the ground on your stomach, or assuming a fetal position to reduce the severity of an attack. Cover the back of your neck with your hands. Do not move until you are certain the bear has left.

✔ Report all bear attacks to the nearest ranger or warden immediately.

✔ If you are attacked at night or if you feel you have been stalked and attacked as prey, try to escape. If you cannot escape, or if the bear follows, use pepper spray, or shout and try to intimidate the bear with a branch or rock. Do whatever it takes to let the bear know you are not easy prey.

There are also ways to avoid attracting a nearby bear's attention. Bears are particularly attracted to odors, so it is important to store food properly and dispose of trash in bear-proof containers. There is safety in numbers, so avoid hiking alone. As former Glacier National Park superintendent Butch Farabee put it following the attack on Craig Dahl in 1998, "Although we cannot prohibit people from hiking alone, we strongly discourage it." (We can attest to this firsthand. A few years ago we were part of a group of perhaps thirty tourists who had come within a few yards of a grizzly sow and cubs near Glacier's Many Glacier Hotel. Although a few of us only saw the bears rustling in the willows, the fact that there were so many of us festooned with bear bells and chatting away anxiously probably gave the sow second thoughts about attacking. Instead the family quietly went about its business.)

Of course, a bear attack can be tragic for both the victim and the bear itself. A bear that attacks because it has become accustomed to being around humans or eating human food simply cannot be tolerated, and most such bears are hunted down and killed. This can have a significant effect on an animal population that numbers in the hundreds rather than the thousands.

It's difficult to believe that the National Park Service in Yellowstone once actively promoted "bear shows," where garbage would be dumped in certain locations for the express purpose of attracting bears for viewing. Naturally, this led to a drastic increase in bear attacks and the subsequent extermination of quite a few bears. Grizzly numbers in particular collapsed. Even though the bear shows were shut down by World War II, tourists in the postwar era expected the Yellowstone experience to include feeding bears from their car windows. By the early 1960s, however, a new way of thinking called for parks to take on a "reasonable illusion of primitive America," and park officials devised ways to keep bears off the roads and in their natural habitat. The garbage dumps were gradually closed in the mid-1970s against the recommendations of biologists John and Frank Craighead, who had spent years studying Yellowstone grizzlies and had concluded that they couldn't sustain a meaningful population without access to at least some garbage. Although the controversy became very public—the Craigheads were widely respected scientists—the Park Service went ahead with its management and recovery plan for Yellowstone's grizzlies regardless. The result has been a grizzly population that has risen from a low of perhaps as few as 136 bears thirty years ago to more than 500 today, and far fewer bear mortalities arising from contact with people.

Rampant Lion: The Cougar

Although they are just now beginning to reappear in their old haunts in America east of the Mississippi, the cougar is still the most widely distributed mammal in the Americas, which might explain why it has been given so many names over the centuries. (For the purposes of this book we have used the appellations cougar, mountain lion, and lion interchangeably.) Cougars, whose official scientific name is *Felis concolor*, today roam from deep into British Columbia all the way south to Patagonia. (Interestingly, the cougar has not found Alaska or northern Canada hospitable, possibly because of competition from bears and wolves, which are abundant. Or perhaps they just don't like prolonged periods of cold and darkness.) Although a firm number is as elusive as the cat itself, the best estimate is that there may be some 30,000 cougars in the United States, including the Florida Panther, a subspecies. It is one of two cats that prey on large mammals in the United States, the other being the jaguar, an occasional interloper into Arizona, New Mexico, and Texas from its principal habitat south of the border.

Curiously, mountain lions have been classified as "small" cats, even though adult males weigh an average of 150 pounds and measure about seven feet from nose to tail, with females averaging 100 pounds and a little over six feet in length. (The tail comprises about one-third of the total length of a cougar.) Cougars are extremely solitary animals and get together only to mate. A typical litter consists of one to three kittens (sometimes referred to as "cubs") after

Cougar (Washington Department of Fish and Wildlife)

a gestation period of about three months. Kittens are born with spotted coats that serve as camouflage until they are big enough to defend themselves; these start to fade after a year or so and give way to the familiar tawny coat of an adult. Kittens can stay with their mother for up to two years, but are often run off by mature males seeking to mate with their mother. (Indeed, males have been known to kill kittens that get in the way of a sexual encounter.)

Although they have been known to eat vegetation and insects, cougars are primarily carnivores, with deer being their prey of choice. However, cougars are extremely opportunistic and will eat anything from porcupines to pine martens. They are not very economical predators, either; a cougar may kill a deer a day just for its liver, leaving the rest of the carcass untouched.

The classic signature of a cougar attack is for it to stalk or surprise its victim, in some cases leaping twenty feet or more to do so. In the case of a large mammal such as a deer or elk, a cougar will usually pounce on the animal's back and try to quickly subdue it by biting into its spinal cord behind the neck. If this fails it may then attempt to rip the throat open. The longer the struggle, it seems, the better the odds are that the prey will escape. Antlers and hooves can be particularly effective in fighting off a cougar, and if a deer or elk gets free it can outrun a cougar in most cases. Though cougars are fast, their endurance is no match for that of many ungulates. Because of this, cougars are not always successful hunters, which explains why in an increasing number of cases near towns and cities they will opt for more accessible prey: dogs, cats, and tragically in rare cases, humans.

The cougar attack that became a wake-up call to suburbia in the western United States was in fact the first ever known case of a lion killing a person in Colorado, and it occurred on January 14, 1991, in the mountain town of Idaho Springs. Idaho Springs is typical of many towns just outside the Denver metropolitan area along I-70; nestled in a valley and straddling Clear Creek, the wildness of the Colorado backcountry is just a short hike away. Indeed, the rugged terrain just behind Idaho Springs High School presents an ideal challenge for a cross-country runner in training, and this is where eighteen-year-old Scott Lancaster found himself on that fateful day. Last seen goofing for classmates as he ran past the high school and toward a steep slope, he was on his second circuit of the run, and he was never seen alive again. His mother contacted several of his friends when he failed to return home that evening, but didn't report him as missing to the authorities until the following morning. A search-and-rescue team that included three dogs didn't find Lancaster's remains until January 16, about a third of a mile from the high school. As Harold P. Danz explains in his excellent book, *Cougar!*, "Given the obvious human bias, there is no way that a cougar attack on a human being can be described as anything but horrifying." Cougars do not issue warning; they attack to kill and eat, and the assault on Scott Lancaster was no exception: in addition to most of his internal organs, the lion had eaten the boy's face and chewed on his neck.

Rescuers noticed a cougar looming about twenty yards away. It was immediately tracked and shot by law enforcement authorities and sent to a Colorado Division of Wildlife laboratory in Fort Collins, where an examination later revealed human hair, bone, and cartilage in its digestive tract. The necropsy further related there was nothing abnormal with the lion's brain, suggesting that the attack on Lancaster was as normal to the cougar as an attack on a deer. (Evidence on the scene also indicated that Lancaster had been attacked from behind.) The cougar was described as a healthy three-year-old male weighing 110 pounds.

The fatal attack on Scott Lancaster seemed to usher in an era of increasing human–cougar encounters that continues to this day. Though Lancaster is believed to have been only the second human killed by a mountain lion in the United States and Canada since 1890, nine such deaths occurred from 1991 to 2006. Five were attacks on children. Non-lethal attacks have also greatly increased, not to mention depredations on pets and livestock.

One of the most compelling stories of someone surviving a cougar attack also occurred in Colorado, seven years after the attack on Scott Lancaster. On April 30, 1998, Andy Peterson was hiking down a trail in Roxborough State Park near Denver when a "burst of purple" caught his eye. As he knelt down to look at the wildflowers that had caught his attention, he felt something wasn't right. Standing up to return to the trail, he saw a mountain lion down the trail sitting under a pine tree and chewing on a stick. At first thrilled at the sight, fear quickly overcame him, and he started slowly walking backward away from the lion. He also reached into his fanny pack and took out a small jackknife. "I knew I had to get past this wild animal in order to get off this mountain," he recalled.

When Peterson next looked up the lion had moved—toward him. Then, "in the blink of an eye," the cougar was in front of him, growling and flattening its ears, telltale signs of an imminent attack. Before Peterson could do anything to defend himself, the lion slammed into his chest, sending both to the ground. After Peterson jumped up, the lion leaped after him again, this time just missing him. Peterson started backpedaling down the trail, waving a shirt in an attempt to distract the lion. Then the cougar just stopped, which gave Peterson time to unbuckle his fanny pack to use as a weapon. With the pack in one hand and his knife in the other, he briefly kept the cougar at bay, then attempted to escape by running down the boulder-strewn trail. The cougar launched into the air and brought him down a second time. After tumbling down the trail with the cougar, Peterson found himself on top of the animal, but the cougar had Peterson's head in its jaws. It bit him hard twice. Peterson tried to retaliate with the knife to no effect. The cougar clawed him on the face and neck. Blood was everywhere.

In trying to fight off the cougar with his hands, Peterson suddenly realized that he could feel the lion's eyes. "Desperately and with all the force I could muster," he later wrote, "I plunged my . . . thumb into its eye, simultaneously sinking the knife into the cat's skull with my left hand." The lion screamed and backed off. Peterson, sporting an eight-inch gash on his head and other wounds, ran for his life. He encountered the lion one more time on the way down, but the fight was out of them both. He collapsed after running for more than two miles, but hikers who had tried to stop him and get him to lie down had already called for help. A helicopter was on the way. Peterson's ordeal with the cougar had lasted nearly thirty minutes, but he had prevailed. (Peterson's remarkable account of the attack is available on his website, *www.lkministries. com*. He concludes the account by stating, "The event you have just read has radically changed my life. I have given my life to the Lord, realizing the importance of having Jesus Christ in my life.")

Is there safety in numbers when traveling through lion country? Not necessarily. On January 8, 2004, a cougar attacked two cyclists who were traveling a popular mountain bike trail in Orange County, California, killing one. Jeffrey Reynolds, riding alone, had apparently stopped to replace the chain on his bike when he was attacked, killed, and partially eaten. Several hours later, Anne Hjelle, riding with a friend, Debbie Nichols, was attacked and dragged into a ravine by the same lion that had killed Reynolds. Nichols tried to pull Hjelle away from the lion in a desperate tug-of-war, while two other cyclists gathered and started pelting the animal with rocks. "This guy would not let go. He had a hold of her face," Nichols later recalled. Only when one of the rocks hit the cougar square in the face did it loosen its grip and flee. Still, the cougar had severely injured Hjelle, ripping away the flesh on her face and neck and tearing her left ear from her head. The cougar was later shot and killed when it returned to the site where Reynolds's body had been found. It was a 110-pound male and about two years old. Tests later confirmed the presence of human flesh in its stomach.

What accounts for the increase in cougar encounters in the western United States? In the case of California, for example, the answer is clear: there are a lot more cougars residing there now than there were thirty years ago. Before then Governor Ronald Reagan imposed a moratorium on the hunting of lions in 1972, for example, there were perhaps six hundred cougars in the state. Today there are about ten times that many.

Yet a more disturbing reason why we may be encountering more cougars today is that they may now consider our backyards viable habitat. The scientist who has given his life to studying the cougar and other big cats, Maurice Hornocker of the University of Idaho, thinks the cougar has definitely changed its ways since he first began studying it fifty years ago. "In those days, I would never have dreamed of the number of encounters between lions and people we see now. They're becoming habituated to people in some areas, and we don't know the reasons why." Those who have studied human–cougar interactions specifically found as early as 1991 that "the number of incidents are on the rise; they are being reported closer to towns and cities; occur year-round rather than just during winter; and more are coming during daylight hours."

In his book *The Beast in the Garden: A Modern Parable of Man and Nature*, a timely examination of evolving attitudes toward increasingly bold cougars in and near Boulder, Colorado, David Baron concludes that "mountain lions are sending a message; they are signaling a change of era, not just to those who have had direct encounters with them but to America as a whole." *Cougar!* author Harold P. Danz contends that "Cougars and humans cannot reside comfortably in the same locale unless there is provision for, and the existence of, varied habitats and abundant space for the cougar to roam. There is just no convenient way [cougars and humans] can share the same closed habitat." Although Danz takes a more traditional view of managing marauding cougars, such as lengthening sport hunting seasons and relocating troublesome cougars out of populated areas, Baron calls for "modifying the behavior" of the cougar as well as some "controls on human actions: where we build our homes, how we landscape our yards, the way we dispose of our trash and house our pets."

Even if implemented right away, none of these suggested actions would have an effect for some time, so those who live in or near cougar country would be wise to follow advice provided by the National Park Service for their safety:

- ✔ Never approach a cougar, especially a feeding one. Cougars are unpredictable individuals, but will normally avoid a confrontation. If you encounter a cougar, be sure to give it a way out.
- ✔ Keep children close to you while hiking, and do not allow them to run ahead or lag behind on the trail. Pick them up if you see fresh signs of a cougar.
- ✔ Hike in a small group. Particularly in areas where cougars have been sighted, avoid hiking alone.
- ✔ Do not jog. People running or moving rapidly may be at higher risk.
- ✔ Carry a walking stick; it makes a useful weapon in the event of an encounter.

If you encounter a cougar:

- ✔ Stop. Do not run.
- ✔ Immediately pick up small children.
- ✔ If you were sitting or bending over, stand upright. Spread your arms, open your coat—try to look as large as possible.
- ✔ Maintain eye contact with the cougar, and attempt to slowly back away.

If a cougar acts aggressively:

- ✔ Be assertive. If approached, wave your arms, shout, and throw sticks or rocks at it.
- ✔ If attacked, fight back aggressively.

A popular misconception is that dogs, particularly large ones, can help deter a cougar attack. The evidence proves otherwise: in one study of thirty-seven dog–cougar interactions, dogs were dominant only 11 percent of the time, and 41 percent of the attacks were fatal to the dog.

Canidae

Of the three general types of wild canines that inhabit the American West, the gray wolf is perhaps the most undeservedly vilified as a danger to humans. Though the gray wolf is a physically formidable animal, averaging over six feet in length and weighing around a hundred pounds, it would rather menace people by preying on their livestock than feasting on their children, as perpetuated in so many fairy tales. Indeed, the last recorded human fatality from a wolf attack occurred in Canada in 2005, after wolves had become habituated to a local garbage dump. (Sound familiar?) This is trivial when set against the number of fatalities from domestic dog attacks in North America over the past twenty-five years: more than three hundred.

Although fatal wolf attacks have occurred with greater frequency in other countries, particularly in India, the wolves that inhabit the western United States are downright docile by comparison. A man who worked on the restoration of wolves to the Yellowstone ecosystem and who subsequently tracked them for ten years, Douglas W. Smith, found that wolves were generally afraid of people, even though "Any one of them, after all, could make short work of any one of us." His own experiences underscored the point: time and again, wolves scurried off whenever his presence was made known, whether he was entering a den to examine pups, prompting the adults to run away, or approaching a kill. Smith hypothesizes that such wary behavior may be due to the fact that we have been killing them for so long. In remote places where wolves have not previously suffered such wanton persecution, Smith notes, wolves often approach humans, but out of curiosity more than aggression.

As Smith also observed, "habituation is slow to develop" in wolves, and the older the wolf, the more wary of humans it becomes. (It is slightly disconcerting that the same things were being said about mountain lions thirty years ago.) In a place like the Yellowstone ecosystem, though, an area that receives more than 3 million visitors and their food and garbage annually, "responsibility for staying separated isn't laid entirely on the wolf." People also must behave. The consequences of not showing responsibility may well be an attack on someone by a wolf habituated to human food, and "all the terror of Little Red Riding Hood—still simmering in parts of our culture—will come flooding back." For safety the park service not only recommends being careful with food while in wolf country, but also keeping your dog on a leash or in the car. And as with cougars, one should never run away from a wolf; that would only be imitating the behavior of its most common prey.

The wolf's smaller cousin, the coyote, has become more of a nuisance than an outright threat to humans, but the combination of its brazenness and our encroachment onto its former habitat has resulted in a steep increase in attacks on humans in recent years. In California alone, for example, federal and local government agencies as well as private wildlife control companies reported eighty-nine coyote attacks on humans for the years 1978 through 2003. This did not include seventy-seven additional incidents where coyotes either "stalked children, chased individuals, or aggressively threatened adults" (see Coyote Attacks in California). (The researchers who collected the data "are also aware of fifteen additional attack incidents involving coyotes and humans in California since the beginning of 2004. There are a number of similar incidents reported from other western states since the mid-1990s, notably Arizona—eighteen incidents, Colorado—three or four incidents, and New Mexico—at least two incidents.)

Coyote attacks in California, 1978–2003, listed chronologically[*]

May 1978 (Pasadena): 5-year-old girl bitten on left leg while in driveway of home.

May 1979 (Pasadena): 2-year-old girl attacked by coyote while eating cookies on front porch; grabbed by throat and cheek.

June 1979 (Pasadena): Adult male bitten on heel while picking up newspaper from front yard.

July 1979 (Pasadena): 17-year-old female's leg lacerated by coyotes while attempting to save dog being attacked.

July 1979 (Pasadena): Coyote bit adult male on legs while jogging; climbed tree to escape.

August 1979 (La Verne): Coyote grabbed 5-year-old girl and attempted to drag her into bushes. Suffered deep bites on neck, head, and legs before saved by father and a neighbor.

July 1980 (Agoura Hills): 13-month-old girl grabbed and dragged off by coyote. Suffered puncture wounds to midsection before being saved by mother.

August 1981 (Glendale): 3-year-old girl killed in front yard by coyote; massive bleeding and broken neck.

August 1988 (Oceanside): 4-year-old boy nipped and bruised by coyote while playing in yard. (Morning)

August 1988 (Oceanside): 8-year-old girl approached by coyote while roller-skating after she had fallen. Coyote tugged at her skate, and was scared off by two women who threw rocks. (Morning)

August 1988 (Oceanside): Coyote grabbed 3-year-old girl by the leg and pulled her down, then bit her on head and neck. Coyote chased off by mother and neighbors. (7 p.m.)

October 1988 (San Diego): Adult female bitten by coyote in backyard while talking on phone. (Daytime)

June 1990 (Reds Meadow): 5-year-old girl attacked and bitten in head while in sleeping bag at campground. (3 a.m.)

*From Trimm, Robert M., Baker, Rex O., Bennett, Joe R. and Coolahan, Craig C., "Coyote Attacks: An increasing Suburban Problem," Transactions, No. American Wildife and Natural Resources Conference 69: 57–68. Also published in Proceedings, Vertebrate Pest Conference, 47–57. Reprinted with permission.

June 1990 (Reds Meadow): One person bitten on foot through sleeping bag; one bitten on hand; same campground as above.

September 1991 (Laguna Niguel): Man chased, and his poodle was ripped from his arms; poodle taken by coyote.

March 1992 (San Marcos): Adult female attacked and bitten on face while rescuing pit bull pup from attack in her yard.

April 1992 (Fallbrook): Grove worker bitten by coyote.

May 1992 (San Clemente): 5-year-old girl attacked and bitten several times on her back, climbed swing set to get away; mother chased off coyote. (Daytime)

October 1992 (Fallbrook): 10-year-old boy attacked and bitten on head while asleep on back porch of residence. (4 a.m.)

October 1994 (Griffith Park): Man with no shirt or shoes bitten by coyote. (5 p.m.)

March 1995 (Griffith Park): Man with no shirt bitten by coyote. (Noon)

March 1995 (Griffith Park): Coyote stalked and then knocked down 5-year-old girl twice; mother rescued child. (Daytime)

June 1995 (Griffith Park): Woman in shorts, barefoot, preparing food, bitten by coyote. (Daytime)

June 1995 (Laguna Niguel): Man attacked while lying on chaise lounge, stargazing bitten on bare foot. (Night)

June 1995 (Laguna Niguel): Man bitten on bare foot while getting newspaper from yard. (Mid-morning)

June 1995 (UC Riverside): Three boys chased; 7-year-old bitten. (Late afternoon)

July 1995 (Griffith Park): Man bitten by coyote while sleeping on lawn. (2:45 p.m.)

July 1995 (Griffith Park): Man bitten by coyote while sleeping on lawn. (4 p.m.)

July 1995 (Griffith Park): Coyote was chased away once; then returned to attack 15-month-old girl in jumpsuit; child suffered bites to leg. (4 p.m.)

September 1995 (Fullerton): 3-year-old girl attacked in yard, bitten on face, head, and thigh. (6:30 p.m.)

November 1995 (UC Riverside): Children chased while playing; 3-year-old boy bitten.

June 1996 (Los Altos): Coyote grabbed 3-year-old boy by hand and dragged him toward bushes; treated for bites on scalp and hand. 15-year-old brother scared coyote away. (8 p.m.)

January 1997 (San Juan Capistrano): Two women attacked; one bitten twice on left ankle and pulled to ground. Both yelled, used alarm device, and swung handbag.

January 1997 (San Juan Capistrano): Coyote attacked adult female, grabbed lunch pail and ran.

January 1997 (San Juan Capistrano): Coyote charged adult female, took purse containing lunch.

January 1997 (San Juan Capistrano): Coyote charged adult female and took purse.

January 1997 (San Juan Capistrano): Coyote attacked man, bit shoe, no injury. Coyote refused to retreat. (Before daylight)

January 1997 (San Juan Capistrano): Coyote jumped on back of man, biting his backpack. Was knocked off and retreated.

February 1997 (South Lake Tahoe): Man attacked and bitten on hand while feeding coyote. (Late morning)

February 1997 (South Lake Tahoe): 4-year-old girl in yard attacked and severely bitten; heavy snowsuit protected all but face. Father rescued child. Coyote stayed in unfenced yard until shot by police. (Late morning)

September 1997 (Pomona): Man was stalked, then attacked by two coyotes, and bitten on ankle. (Early evening, daylight)

November 1998 (San Mateo County): Coyote approached group of 4 women hikers and bit woman on buttocks.

November 1998 (San Mateo County): Coyote approached 3 women hikers, grabbed one by her pant leg, let go, attempted to attack again.

Spring 1999 (South Lake Tahoe area): Two adults bitten by coyotes.

Spring 1999 (South Lake Tahoe area): Woman bitten by coyote in parking lot of motel.

May 1999 (Canyon Country): Coyote attacked dog in yard, and would not cease attack; man scratched in melee. (Night)

August 1999 (Green Valley Lake): Coyotes attacked woman and her dogs in yard; one dog bitten. Woman and dogs escaped to vehicle; coyotes jumped aggressively on car and scratched it. (8:30 a.m.)

August 1999 (San Antonio Heights): Three coyotes attacked and killed dog being walked on leash by elderly man.

October 1999 (Ventura County): Six coyotes attacked man on bicycle with his dog; dog bitten.

November 1999 (Hollywood Hills): Coyote attacked and killed pet dog in man's presence; coyote would not leave. (Morning)

February 2000 (Calimesa): Adult male attacked in backyard by coyote while attempting to rescue dog; suffered cuts, scrapes, and bruises. (9 p.m.)

May 2000 (La Mesa): 3-year-old boy bitten on his side; treated for 4 puncture wounds. (7 p.m.)

May 2000 (Dublin area): Coyote killed small dog while woman was taking it for walk.

October 2000 (Oildale): Pair of coyotes treed woman's pet cat, then turned aggressively on her.

April 2001 (Pomona): 54-year-old woman fought, using an axe handle, with a large coyote that had attacked small poodle in backyard. Received bite on leg, and despite her efforts, the coyote killed the poodle and jumped over fence carrying the carcass. (4:30 p.m.)

June 2001 (Frazier Park): 22-year-old female camp counselor sleeping in open awakened by coyote sniffing and pawing at her head. (2 a.m.)

June 2001 (Northridge): 7-year-old girl attacked and seriously injured by a coyote, despite mother's attempts to fight off the coyote. (7 p.m.)

July 2001 (Thousand Oaks): Five coyotes attacked large dog in yard, and aggressively threatened residents attempting to rescue dog; would not leave area despite two visits by sheriff.

July 2001 (Irvine): 3-year-old boy bitten by coyote in leg while playing in yard; attack interrupted by father, who was 10-20 feet away at time of bite. (8:15 p.m.)

July 2001 (Tustin): Coyote bit woman.

July 2001 (Encinitas): Coyote attacked and took dog, while it was being walked on leash by woman. (4 p.m.)

August 2001 (Hollywood Hills): Coyotes bit man 8 times as he was defending his dog against their attack. (11:50 p.m.)

August 2001 (Irvine): Woman walking poodle on leash bitten by coyote while attempting to remove dog from coyote's mouth. (4:30 p.m.)

August 2001 (Chatsworth): Two coyotes came into yard and took pet cat out of hands of 19-month-old toddler.

September 2001 (Agoura): Woman attacked by coyote when she attempted to stop its attack on her small dog. (7:15 a.m.)

September 2001 (Lancaster): Man walking encountered 4 coyotes, which crouched, circling him, attempting to attack. Fought off with walking stick, hitting one square across the face. (Morning)

October 2001 (San Clemente): Coyote attacked children on schoolyard; 8-year-old girl bitten on back of neck and scratched; 7-year-old boy bitten on back and arm. Third student attacked but coyote bit backpack. (12:15 p.m.)

November 2001 (San Diego): 8-year-old girl bitten in leg by coyote that family had been feeding at their apartment. (1:30 p.m.)

November 2001 (La Habra Heights): Coyote on golf course ran up to woman, jumped on her back, and bit her on right forearm. (Daytime).

December 2001 (San Gabriel): Coyote bit 3-year-old girl in head; grabbed her shoulder in an attempt to drag her off. Father chased coyote off. (7:30 p.m.)

May 2002 (Anza Borrego St. Park): Coyote bit boy in sleeping bag on the head.

May 2002 (Los Angeles): Coyote attacked man walking his dog.

July 2002 (Woodland Hills): Adult female attacked by coyote, bitten on arm. (6 a.m.)

July 2002 (Woodland Hills): Adult male bitten on boot by coyote when he inadvertently came upon it between car and garage.

July 2002 (Canoga Park): Woman walking 2 large dogs accosted by 3 coyotes; fell backward and fended coyotes off.

July 2002 (Carlsbad): Woman walking Labrador retriever accosted by 8–10 coyotes, which bit at her legs and pants after she tripped and fell; her dog fought off the coyotes until she could escape. (10 p.m.)

August 2002 (Mission Hills): Coyote approached couple walking dog, attempting to snatch dog out of man's arms; left only after being kicked. (4 a.m.)

November 2002 (Carbon Canyon): Coyote came into trailer park and took dog in presence of its owner. (3 p.m.)

November 2002 (Woodland Hills): Coyote scaled 6-foot wall into yard, attacked and killed small dog in presence of owner; in melee, woman kicked coyote, then fell and fractured her elbow and was attacked and scratched by coyote. (1 p.m.)

December 2002 (East Highland): Utility worker attacked by coyote, which tore his trousers. (Evening)

December 2002 (East Highland): Coyote attacked adult male. (Evening)

February 2003 (Lake View Terrace): Jogger bitten (tooth scrape on ankle) by coyote after jogging past neighborhood coyote feeding station.

May 2003 (Woodland Hills): Coyote acted aggressively toward man after he intervened during its attack on his dog.

May 2003 (Highland): Coyote came into neighbor's garage after 2-year-old girl, biting her on arm. (10 p.m.)

May 2003 (Woodland Hills): Coyote came into residence to attack small pet dogs. (2 p.m.)

July 2003 (Granada Hills): Boy walking family's 2 dogs attacked by 3 coyotes; one dog was killed and the other injured; rescued by father.

July 2003 (Alta Loma): Coyote grabbed her small dog while woman was walking it; she was able to rescue it.

August 2003 (Apple Valley): 4-year-old boy attacked on golf course; bitten on face and neck; saved by father. (Late afternoon)

November 2003 (Claremont): Man and his dog attacked by 3–4 coyotes; he defended himself, hitting several coyotes with his walking stick. (8 a.m.)

Coyotes are smaller than wolves, although large coyotes can be confused with small wolves, making for frequent cases of mistaken identity by unwitting visitors to places like Yellowstone or Alaska. A male coyote averages three and a half to four feet in length and weighs about twenty-five pounds. Females are slightly smaller and lighter. A normal litter consists of from five to seven pups, but a den may contain two litters given the polygynous nature of males. This fact, as well as the coyote's reputation as a fearless, opportunistic scavenger, helps explain why they are so common. Coyotes range from Alaska south to Costa Rica, and, as previously mentioned, are now returning to the Midwest and East Coast of the United States.

In the wild, coyotes are universal carnivores, though about 15 percent of what they eat consists of vegetative matter. Carrion of large mammals is preferred, but coyotes also hunt and kill small animals, from gophers to ground-nesting birds. However, coyotes in urban and suburban areas are more than happy to change their diets to take advantage of what's readily available, and will alter their "natural" behavior accordingly. Scat analysis of urban- and suburban-dwelling coyotes in California found everything from house cats to zucchini, and, of course, a fair amount of garbage. Coyotes in the wild seldom hunt in packs, but they have been known to attack in numbers once they've become habituated to humans. (In July 2002 a woman walking her Labrador retriever in Carlsbad, California, was attacked by "eight to ten" coyotes. The Lab managed to drive them off.)

The principal culprit in coyote attacks on humans in suburbia—coyotes seldom, if ever, attack people in the wild—is carelessness with food and house pets. Though dozens of people are bitten or at least harassed by coyotes every year, the only recent fatal attack occurred in August 1981, when three-year-old Kelly Lynn Keen was dragged from her home in Glendale, California, a suburb of Los Angeles. Kelly's father Robert ran to her rescue and chased the coyote off, but she later died from her wounds after undergoing four hours of surgery at Glendale Adventist Hospital. Keen's children had been approached by coyotes on two occasions prior to the attack on Kelly, and in both instances Robert had shot the animals because he was "dissatisfied with the city's program to curb the [coyote] problem."

The varied reactions to the death of Kelly Keen typified the mixed feelings of a community that is both wary and appreciative of wild animals in their midst. On the one hand, local officials, whose job it was to ensure the residents of Glendale's safety, sought ways to trap and kill marauding coyotes by sharing the cost to do so with people who wished to have them removed. On the other hand, animal rights activists found trapping and killing inhumane. A biology professor from Pomona College even went so far as to say that the coyotes were helping bring balance to the ecosystem. Without coyotes, he maintained, "residents of urban areas would suffer serious vegetable and ornamental plant losses to rodents and rabbits." Suffice to say that when a scientist mentions suburban gardens and "ecosystem" in the same breath that there is much confusion about what we loosely call "nature." As David Baron concludes in *The Beast in the Garden*, "Edward Abbey, repeating a comment by friend and fellow eco-warrior Doug Peacock, once wrote 'It ain't wilderness . . . unless there's a critter out there that can kill and eat you.' That may be true, but the inverse is not; just because there's a critter out there that can kill and eat you doesn't mean it *is* wilderness."

Antlers, Hooves, and Bad Tempers

In a way that you normally wouldn't think of, the members of the deer family (deer, elk, and moose) are among the most dangerous animals in North America. In 2003 alone, for example, there were an estimated 1.5 million vehicle collisions with deer that killed 201 people and cost insurers $1.1 billion. In over a third of the fatal collisions, drivers died from injuries after falling from a stricken motorcycle or ATV. Another third died when their cars veered off the road and either rolled or struck some fixed object. The Insurance Institute for Highway Safety estimates that many of the fatalities may have been avoided if people had simply been wearing helmets or seat belts. Unfortunately, if the animal is the much larger elk or moose, then even these precautions may not be enough to avoid death or serious injury. (Indeed, because of the prevalence of moose–vehicle crashes in Sweden, both Saab and Volvo simulate such collisions when crash-testing their vehicles.) Of course, such accidents are not so good for the animals, either; the Pennsylvania Game Commission reported an astounding 41,534 deer were killed by motor vehicles in 1991 alone.

In these incidents, however, the animals' behavior can be said to have been somewhat benign, and with their death rates many thousands times that of humans in such accidents, they are more the victims of aggression than vice versa. But that doesn't mean members of the deer family are incapable of aggression against humans; add in those all-too-familiar circumstances of habituation, interference with young, and even an ill-timed flashbulb and any ungulate is capable of charging a person. During the summer of 2004 a marauding mule deer buck continually harassed anglers along the Madison River in Montana, and even attacked an eighty-year-old man outside his home in Cameron in what amounted to a sneak attack from behind. The victim, Gene Novikoff, was only able to escape when the buck became mesmerized by its own reflection in Novikoff's recently cleaned SUV. Novikoff then scrambled back to his house, grabbed his .22, and shot the deer six times so he could get to his car. The deer merely ran off, unharmed. The game warden who investigated the incidents, Marc Glines of the Montana Department of Fish, Wildlife, and Parks postulated the deer may have been raised as a pet by someone because it showed no fear of humans.

Bull elk, or wapiti, which stand about five feet at the shoulder and weigh 750 pounds, can be particularly feisty during the "rut" or autumn mating season. One unlucky visitor to Yellowstone found

Bull elk with its formidable antlers on full display. (National Park Service, Yellowstone National Park)

this out the hard way in September 2004. A bull elk was minding its own business one Sunday morning near the Terrace Grill in Yellowstone's Mammoth Hot Springs, when a sixty-year-old Texas man came within ten feet to take the elk's picture. (Park regulations advise people to stay at least twenty-five yards away from elk and other large animals.) Evidently the flash from the camera surprised the elk, which then charged and struck the man, causing injuries to his head, chest, and hands. But that was just the beginning of the animal's rampage. It later charged a park employee and attacked a dozen parked cars, causing from $12,000 to $15,000 in damage. Park officials then took the unusual step of tranquilizing the elk and cutting off its antlers. Though Yellowstone spokesman Al Nash noted that this elk's aggressive behavior was abnormal, he also said, "This just reinforces that we need to keep people at a safe distance. These animals are beautiful and we love them, but seven hundred pounds of elk with a big rack is something to be respected."

By far the most imposing and aggressive members of the deer family are moose, which injure more people in Alaska than do bears. The species common to the intermountain West from Colorado north to the Canadian border is the Shiras moose, smaller than Yukon–Alaska moose but still the largest big-game animal in the lower forty-eight states. An adult male can measure nearly six feet at the shoulder, weigh a thousand pounds, and grow antlers over six feet in width. In an astoundingly successful reintroduction program, twelve moose were transplanted from Utah to Colorado's North Park in 1978; by 1992 the moose were doing so well that some were moved to the upper Rio Grande drainage in southern Colorado. Wildlife officials in Colorado today estimate that one thousand moose inhabit the state, and limited hunting is now offered in North Park and Middle Park and the Laramie River basin. A male moose even spent the summer of 2007 grazing along the I-25 corridor north of Denver. It eluded capture until wildlife officials cornered it near Highway 36 in suburban Broomfield in September.

Though they tend to be loners (a cow with calves being the exception), moose can appear to be generally indifferent to the presence of humans, which is probably why people tend to be complacent about their safety in moose country. In fact, moose can "snap" at any time, for any reason. A cow moose may attack to protect her

The deceptively docile, dangerous moose. (National Park Service, Yellowstone National Park)

young. A bull moose can become particularly aggressive during the rut. An old, tired, and hungry moose may attack out of sheer frustration. In March 2004 three snowshoers came face-to-face with an eight-hundred-pound moose on a trailhead just ten miles east of Salt Lake City. At first the moose just "stared them down" for a few minutes as the three men slowly backed away, but then the moose suddenly crashed through the brush and started stomping on Nick Baldwin, age sixty-five. Baldwin's companions threw sticks and managed to eventually drive the animal off, but not before it had injured

Baldwin's right leg and head. Because the moose was still nearby, the three men climbed a tree to safety and used a cell phone to call 911. Forty minutes later, a Division of Wildlife Resources officer arrived, but because the moose stood between him and the men in the tree, the officer had to bring it down with a tranquilizer gun so he could get to the injured Baldwin. Baldwin was evacuated by helicopter, and the moose left the area once the tranquilizer wore off.

Moose are particularly sensitive to their "space," and they need lots of it. Those who study moose behavior advise people to always yield to a moose by backing off or changing direction in the event of an unexpected encounter. (Of course, if you are between a cow and her calf, you might already be in danger.) Though they may appear docile, even resting moose can become agitated if approached too closely. And because moose are "programmed" to attack their mortal enemy, the wolf, any canine relative is fair game. Dogs should never accompany hikers in moose country.

As with bears, moose can bluff a charge, but that's no reason to stand one's ground. Moose can run (as fast as 30 miles per hour), but it's still possible to run away from a moose because they usually don't run very far. (Indeed, one reason they tend to attack rather than flee is that they don't have the "breakaway" running ability of an elk or deer.)

The best way to defend against a moose attack—assuming a moose doesn't already have you on the ground—is to climb a tree and wait for the moose to leave the area. If a moose does knock you down, curl up in a ball and protect your head with your hands and arms. If a moose stops stomping, that doesn't necessarily mean the attack is over. Stay curled up until the moose is a safe distance away.

Befitting an ecosystem that has the largest free-ranging herd of bison, Yellowstone also averages about three bison attacks a year, and once again most of the victims are people who have approached the 1,500-pound beasts too closely. Indeed, a study conducted from 1978 to 2000 found that, based on the number of encounters, bison were by far the most dangerous wild animals in the ecosystem. Although there were thirty grizzly attacks resulting in two fatalities over the two-decade period, bison attacked people on eighty-one occasions, with one fatality occurring in 1984. (The previous fatality was in 1971.) As the *Billings Gazette* reported, researchers concluded:

The high toll may be due to the public perception of bison, biologists said. While most people respect or even fear bears, many do not think of shaggy and lumbering bison as dangerous.

"I think when they see a bear out there, they're less likely to approach it than they are a bison, which they sort of treat like a big domestic cow," said Yellowstone grizzly bear biologist Kerry Gunther.

A bison normally attacks (or, to its mind, defends) by lowering its head in an attempt to gore with its horns; consequently, most human injuries occur in the abdomen, buttocks, or legs.

Much as we tend to get worked up over the near decimation of the humpback whale from Pacific waters but ignore the equally endangered Alabama lampmussel (a type of clam), so, too, do we seem to view injuries from small, repulsive-looking, but still dangerous creatures as somehow not on par with an attack by a large, ferocious mammal. The truth is, the smaller the critter, the deadlier the animal, whether it's a mosquito carrying West Nile disease or a rattlesnake lying in wait near a golf course. To cite two examples, the American West contains 158 kinds of snakes, many of which are venomous, and 86 species of scorpions, 2 of which are venomous (though they can all bite). Still, though Americans suffer some 8,000 snake bites a year, most such incidents do not merit so much as a mention in the police notes, whereas even a benign encounter with a grizzly bear may grab headlines. Even in this book we have focused on animals that people want to read about and not less attractive (but no less deadly) species of snakes, insects, and even plants.

This phenomenon is clear to anyone who has deliberately chosen to live in cougar or bear country. In an essay published in 1999, journalist and *The Perfect Storm* author Sebastian Junger aptly describes "adventure" as a "situation where the outcome is not entirely within your control." Coming upon a cougar on a trail or even in your backyard certainly qualifies as a situation where the outcome may not be under your control. (One would presumably have more control over a situation that involved a snake or an insect.) As Junger further explains, this is not necessarily an undesirable predicament, for "Modern society ... has perfected the art of having nothing happen at all." Because life for most Americans has become "staggeringly easy," he suggests, "it has also become vaguely unfulfilling." Anyone looking for support for Junger's view need only open the pages of a magazine such as *Outside* to get a sense of all of the manufactured, voluntary, and thoroughly recreational perils we have created for ourselves.

Indeed, it is common for people who live with wild and potentially dangerous animals in their midst to be conflicted in the aftermath of an attack. As David Baron recounts in *The Beast in the Garden*, for example, the Colorado Division of Wildlife "braced itself for a backlash ... against the agency, and against lions in general" in the wake of the fatal cougar attack on Scott Lancaster in 1991. However, "It never came ... people ... did not blame the agency for the fatal attack, and Coloradans did not rise up against cougars." In fact, among Lancaster's friends and family "a consensus emerged that his death, sad and untimely though it was, had somehow been acceptable."

One hundred years ago, such an attack might have provoked an extermination campaign against cougars. The irony of life in the modern American West is that the more comfortable we have become, the more risk we've been willing to take, if only for the sake of "adventure."

II

MISSING

Any parent who has lost a child in the grocery store, if only temporarily, knows the sense of sheer terror in those initial minutes when the toddler seems to have suddenly vanished from the face of the earth. Though the disappearance of an older child or adult may not elicit the same feeling of panic, hope dims as time goes on and no rational explanation presents itself. The vastness and inherent danger of many areas of the American West provide many opportunities for even the most wilderness savvy hiker to go missing. Many who have never returned have simply become victims of some calamity, such as a debilitating fall, lightning strike, or flash flood. Bodies may not be discovered for weeks, even years, if at all. And then there are those who go deliberately missing: with an average population density of thirty-five people per square mile, and with three states registering population densities in the single digits—Wyoming, Montana, and North Dakota all have population densities of fewer than ten people per square mile—the West is a good place for the ne'er-do-well or willful hermit to lose himself.

Missing person stories begin as mysteries, puzzles to be solved. The ones with the worst possible outcomes become death investigations. Some turn out to be amazing stories of survival after enduring some impossible ordeal; Aron Ralston's incredible story of being pinned by a rock near Canyonlands National Park in 2003—and his subsequent self-amputation to free himself—comes to mind. Finally, there are some missing person stories that will have no resolution—they will simply remain mysteries. The accounts that follow are dramatic examples of all three of these possible outcomes, each carrying with it a reminder that the American West of 2008 can be no less dangerous than the American West of 1808. As one contemporary writer has observed, there are still places in the West where you can see "to the edge of forever." For some, reaching the edge of forever has meant entering the portal to eternity.

Laura

At any one time, according to statistics kept by the FBI, there can be close to 900,000 people reported missing in the United States, including runaways, victims of abduction, "throwaways," or just plain lost. Overwhelmingly, children comprise the majority of missing person reports, for the obvious reasons that they are both the most exploitable and vulnerable. Of the 876,213 people reported as missing from 1999 to 2000, for example, 797,500—91 *percent*— were children. The kidnapping and brutal murder of nine-year-old Amber Hagerman in Arlington, Texas, in 1997 led to the development of "AMBER Alerts," television and radio announcements similar to severe weather bulletins announcing that a child is missing. Many successful recoveries of missing children have occurred as a direct result of this program, but for Mike Bradbury of Huntington Beach, California, and his family, the Amber Alert program came along ten years too late.

The Bradburys were a family whose travails would have tested anyone. Three years after marrying in 1969, Mike and Patty Bradbury moved to Anchorage, Alaska, where they found success in the raw gold jewelry manufacturing business, eventually doing business with the likes of Neiman Marcus and other hi-brow stores. Together they brought home over $100,000 a year, a lot of money for 1972. However, the stress and strain eventually took its toll on Mike's health, and after an eye-opening heart attack he moved the family to Huntington Beach, California. By this time he and Patty had a son, Travis, and a daughter, Laura. Mike became an expert on caning, opened a wicker shop, and though the money was nowhere near as good as it had been in the jewelry business, he enjoyed being able to take his family to the beach anytime.

Another daughter, Emily, was born in 1984 and diagnosed with a cleft palate and a heart condition. Medical bills further compromised the family's already frugal lifestyle, and they started to feel the walls of their small condominium closing in. In mid-October they decided to escape to Joshua Tree National Monument for a break, as they had annually since Travis was born eight years earlier.

Located one hundred miles east of Los Angeles, what is now Joshua Tree National Park showcases the best of California's Mojave and Colorado deserts, its name taken for the oddly shaped trees that dot the landscape like so many arboreal scarecrows. Equally imposing are the formations of quartz monzonite at the park's west end, monoliths rising from the desert floor to as much as 150 feet in height. Home to desert bighorn sheep as well as the West's ubiq-

Sparse vegetation and these monolithic quartz monzonite rock formations define the landscape of Joshua Tree National Park. Given the relatively barren landscape, it's difficult to understand how someone could simply vanish here. (National Park Service, Joshua Tree National Park)

uitous coyotes and mule deer, flora and fauna must adapt to extremes
of heat and cold and a general lack of water. Calling it a "seduc-
tive blend of beauty and mystery," one writer has commented that
"good people go there to relax, misfits go there to hide."

The Bradburys arrived at Indian Cove Campground at the north
entrance of Joshua Tree at about 3:35 p.m. on October 18. While
Laura and Travis played nearby and Patty held Emily, Mike hastily
set up camp. Laura, a brown-eyed blonde measuring about three
feet tall at the time, was happily padding about in her multicolored
flip-flops, purple shorts, and green sweatshirt. When Travis decided
he needed to use one of the chemical toilets eighty yards from the
campsite, Laura followed. Travis would later recall hearing her prat-
tling outside the toilet, then hearing the door slam on the adjacent
women's toilet. When Travis emerged from the toilet Laura was nowhere to be found, so he assumed she had gone back to the campsite. However, when Mike asked, "Where's Laura?" upon Travis's
return, instant panic set in.

Mike immediately took off for the toilets, leaving Patty bewildered
and calling out urgently, "What's wrong? What's wrong?" Finding
no sign of Laura in or near the toilets, he began scouring the sparse
vegetation while Patty drove around the campground calling Laura's
name. By this time, fellow campers had joined the search, but their
efforts proved futile, and after an hour one of the campers notified
Park Service officials. What made Laura's complete disappearance
all the more baffling was the fact that the Indian Cove campsite
was in a ten-square-mile area bounded by solid rock walls on three
sides and a highway on the fourth. Had she wandered toward the
highway she would have most certainly been seen by someone. But
she had not. She had simply vanished.

In one of the greatest search-and-rescue efforts ever mounted by
the National Park Service and local authorities, 270 people or more
descended on the area within hours. At their disposal were military
helicopters, computers, specially trained dogs, and heat-detecting
electronic devices sophisticated enough to distinguish between body
heat and warm rocks. Still, all this effort and technology didn't yield
so much as a thread from Laura's clothing. Some small footprints
were found, but because they led directly back to the campground,
it was determined that they couldn't have been Laura's. After

seventy-two hours the search was called off, and the case was taken up by the San Bernardino County Sheriff's Department.

The sheriff department's investigation was led by Gene Bowlin, a twenty-five-year veteran of the force and captain of the sheriff's Morongo Basin Station. Bowlin brought together a force of fifty investigators who would track down every known sex offender in the area, solicit tips, and even consult psychics. Putting in twelve- to fourteen-hour days, the investigators even scrutinized the Bradburys themselves, subjecting both parents to polygraph tests. A $25,000 "no strings attached" reward was even offered, and Laura's face appeared on grocery bags and milk cartons nationwide—the first ever such use of both to aid in the search of a missing child.

After nearly eighteen months of fruitless leads, a discovery was made that, for a time, was viewed with great skepticism: in March 1986 a Marine master sergeant hiking two miles northwest of the Indian Cove campsite had come across a piece of human skullcap. Though an effort to determine sex and blood type proved inconclusive, a forensic anthropologist determined that the piece of skull was from a child between two and five years of age, and that the child had been dead less than five years. With this information, the San Bernardino sheriff postulated that Laura might have wandered on to the unstable lip of a dry wash, which collapsed and buried her. Rain and wind then might have uncovered her body, hastening decomposition and exposure to wild animals and leaving all but the piece of skull.

Mike Bradbury would have none of this theory, and wouldn't even accept that the skullcap was Laura's. By this time, Mike was also frustrated by what he perceived as the growing incompetence of the San Bernardino County sheriff in handling the case, so he began to take the investigation into his own hands. He sold his late mother's diamond wedding ring and bought a computer with a large memory to search vast databases for possible suspects. When Bowlin refused to issue a warrant for the arrest of one possible suspect, Bradbury conducted his own surveillance of the man, both from the ground and the air, but all he accomplished was to force the suspect to move away. Mike Bradbury founded the Laura Center, a foundation dedicated to finding missing children, which started receiving contributions. Notwithstanding reports to the contrary, the

Bradburys were not exploiting their daughter's disappearance to get rich, as evidenced by their beat-up 1972 Volkswagen van as well as the fact that Mike had to give up his job so he could spend full-time performing background checks on possible suspects. However, sensing hostility from those involved in the case—both inside and outside the law—he did arm himself with a shotgun and two rifles.

Over time, leads dried up, support for the Laura Center waned, and many who had dedicated months and even years to finding Laura had moved on. Still, nearly three years after Laura's disappearance Mike was convinced she was still alive. Moreover, "Because the San Bernardino County Sheriff's Department can't or won't find her," according to a lengthy article in the *Los Angeles Times Magazine*, "the only explanation that makes sense to [Bradbury] is an interlocking conspiracy including top Sheriff's department officials, judges, attorneys, drug dealers, and pedophiles."

Ultimately, the advancement of forensic science would confirm Laura's fate. DNA testing in late 1989 on the mysterious piece of skullcap found almost four years earlier near Indian Cove campground confirmed it was in all likelihood Laura's. The tests were sufficiently conclusive for the authorities to close the case on Laura Bradbury's disappearance. The Bradburys, who by this time had closed the Laura Center and moved out of the area in the interests of the remaining children, would not—or could not—comment on the test results, though Laura's grandfather did say, "We don't have any choice but to accept it." Still, questions remain. If Laura had indeed never left the Indian Cove Campground, then why was she not discovered in the initial search, one that involved nearly three hundred people and enough equipment to field an army battalion? Had she been kidnapped, or dragged away by a mountain lion, only to have her remains re-deposited on the desert floor barely two miles from the Bradburys' campsite? In the end, the only explanation that holds up is that of the much-maligned San Bernardino County sheriff: she had somehow fallen and been buried by the collapsing lip of a dry wash.

The desert had swallowed her.

The Iceman

In 1987 Eric LeMarque achieved something that only a handful of fellow Southern Californians had done: he was selected in the tenth round of the National Hockey League draft by the Boston Bruins. Back then, Los Angeles was hardly a breeding ground for hockey players on any level, but LeMarque, who had been born in Paris and claimed dual French–U.S. citizenship, was introduced to the sport at an early age and quickly developed the skills that would ultimately make him attractive to the Bruins. After playing club hockey in the LA area—his high school did not offer the sport—LeMarque played with the semiprofessional Saskatoon Blades in Saskatchewan, and then later for the University of Northern Michigan, where his play caught the eye of Bruins' scouts.

Still, LeMarque was not a huge man at five-ten and 185 pounds, and it was uncertain whether his "finesse" style of play could adapt to the very physical play of the National Hockey League. Indeed, after failing to make the cut with the Bruins, he played pro hockey in Europe for five years, and by virtue of his French citizenship played his way on to the French national team for the 1994 Olympics in Lillehammer. No match for powerhouses Canada, Sweden, Germany, and Finland, the French failed to win a game, and afterward LeMarque retired from professional hockey and returned to Los Angeles, where he worked in sales and kept in shape by coaching hockey and snowboarding.

On February 2, 2004, LeMarque joined a group of friends at Mammoth Mountain resort in the Sierra Nevada for a week of snowboarding and skiing. After his friends departed on February 6, LeMarque decided to go for one more snowboarding run on the 11,000-foot-high mountain. For all his friends knew, Eric might have been still relaxing in his condo, for he failed to tell anyone of his intentions—a classic mistake.

Late in the afternoon on the day of February 6, the thirty-four-year-old LeMarque was atop Mammoth Mountain looking for a "fresh line" of virgin powder for his last run. Not finding desirable conditions on the front side of the mountain, where most of the resort's normal runs were located, Eric climbed a ridge known as Dragon's Back just shy of the summit, where he spotted a slope of untracked powder that was outside the ski area's boundary. After what he called a "fantastic powder run," during which he had passed a saddle that would have taken him back to the front of the mountain, he proceeded to walk in what he thought was the right direction. As it turned out, he was headed away from the resort, plunging himself southward into the 231,000-acre Ansel Adams Wilderness. And the sun was going down, quickly.

When LeMarque realized that he would not make it to the resort

Just beyond the groomed slopes of Mammoth lies a wilderness. (Courtesy Mammoth Mountain Ski Area)

before dark, he resigned himself to spending the night in the wilderness. He took stock of his provisions: four sticks of bubble gum, a cell phone with a dead battery, the keys to his condominium, an MP3 player, and a pack of soggy matches. Finding shelter, he dug a fire pit and attempted to burn some of his clothes in the hope that the plume of smoke would be seen by the ski patrol. But the matches would not ignite. When he saw a pair of coyotes in the distance, he feared they would smell his bubble gum and attack him, so he swallowed the gum that was in his mouth and threw the rest away. Slightly panicked and thinking, "God, I've got to get out of here," LeMarque strapped on his board and slid downhill—farther away from Mammoth.

In the days that followed, LeMarque continued to board downhill, ever farther away from safety, in search of a road. He survived by eating bark and making a makeshift sleeping bag from his parka. (He would use his snowboard to scrape pine boughs off trees to use as a crude mattress.) At one point he decided that hopping rocks in a riverbed was easier than slogging through the twelve-foot-deep snow, until he fell in the freezing water. The force of the current on his snowboard nearly took him over an eighty-foot waterfall. Wet and cold, he stripped the clothes off his back and attempted to dry them on the sun-soaked surface of a boulder. Removing his boots and socks, he saw that his feet were already black and purple and red. Cleverly, at one point either three or four days into his ordeal (he can't remember which) he turned on the radio on his MP3 player to use as a direction finder. When the signal from a radio station in Mammoth grew stronger when pointed in a direction he hadn't expected, he realized he had been walking in the wrong direction. He turned in the direction of the signal and gingerly climbed up 1,200 feet until he reached a mountain called Pumice Butte, where he built a snow shelter. This was his fifth day out, and by now the single-digit cold, wind, and hunger had completely sapped his energy. He had lost thirty-five pounds. Even if he had a little energy left, he couldn't have hiked any farther. "I couldn't get a boot on," he later told the *Los Angeles Times*. "I was walking in the snow with one foot in the boot, with socks on either foot. One foot was by itself in the snow. . . . I found myself trying to walk, falling over."

Compounding all of LeMarque's problems, no one realized he was missing until Wednesday, February 11. His parents had grown concerned when they hadn't heard from him in several days, so Eric's father Philip drove to Mammoth five days after Eric became lost to inspect his condominium. It was what Philip *didn't* find that was disturbing: missing were Eric's keys to the condo, his snowboard, and his season pass to Mammoth. That could mean only one thing: he was somewhere near the mountain, either dead, injured, or lost. But how long had he been gone? Where was he?

The Mono County Sheriff's Search and Rescue team swung into action the next day. They queried LeMarque's friends, who indicated they had last seen him on February 6, but that knowledge still couldn't confirm how long Eric had been gone. If he had indeed been missing for five days, chances of finding him alive were slim. The first day of searching turned up nothing. Though no snow had fallen since February 6, searchers could find no tracks on the snow-covered main road from Mammoth Mountain to the San Joaquin National Forest.

Two more skiers were reported missing the following day, calling for an expanded search of the Mammoth area. (Later that day the skiers walked into a nearby resort, having discovered the route back that LeMarque had missed on his first day out.) The date was Friday, February 13, and LeMarque had determined that he would either die or be saved before the sun went down. With the weather cooperating, searchers caught a break and found a snowboard trail that led to LeMarque's fire pit he had made his first day out. "We weren't sure if it was someone leaving a marker or it was just kindling," a member of the ski patrol recalled, "but we kind of had a hunch that we were onto something." Still, since it was generally believed that LeMarque might have been missing for as long as seven days, searchers were fairly certain they were looking for a body, not a survivor.

Following another snowboard trail that led away and downhill from the fire pit, after nine miles the searchers came across Rainbow Falls, and correctly surmised that LeMarque had decided to follow the river at that point because the snowboard trail resumed downstream. Reasonably certain that LeMarque (or his body) had to be in the area, the search-and-rescue team called for a helicopter to complete the search. Using infrared imaging, the helicopter crew found LeMarque at about 3:30, but were shocked at what they saw: a semiconscious man on his knees, waving frantically. "It amazed everybody," Bill Greene of Mono County Sheriff Search and Rescue told *Newsweek*. "I don't think anybody was not surprised to see him alive."

LeMarque had been resourceful, smart, and lucky. His years of training for professional and Olympic hockey no doubt prepared him well for the seven-day ordeal. He took advantage of the few resources he had, such as using his MP3 player as a compass and his snowboard as a hatchet and shovel to fell pine boughs and dig a snow shelter. Finally, the weather had held just long enough for his tracks to remain uncovered over the seven days he was lost. Two days after he was rescued, more than a hundred inches of snow fell on Mammoth over a period of two to three weeks.

LeMarque had survived, but just barely. After receiving some preliminary treatment at a medical facility in Mammoth, he was taken to the Grossman Burn Center at Sherman Oaks Hospital to have his massive cases of frostbite treated. At one point, he contracted a severe fever, raising his temperature to a dangerous 107 degrees Fahrenheit. Ever the optimist, Eric at first claimed he could wiggle his toes, but according to Dr. Peter Grossman, "What was happening was the muscles for moving his toes were up in his calf. . . . I stuck a pin in his foot, and he had no sensation." Surgeons shortly thereafter amputated LeMarque's feet just below the ankles. They later had to amputate his legs below the knees to accommodate prosthetic legs and feet. Vowing to return to snowboarding the following season, LeMarque began the painful process of learning how to walk again.

Missing: Deliberately

It was an episode in the recent history of the American West that might have come from the imaginations of the film world's Coen brothers, except that it actually happened. It paralyzed a vast section of Colorado and Utah for several weeks during one long, hot, summer; martial law, though undeclared, was implicit in several small towns where heavily armed federal agents swarmed in Blackhawk helicopters. It inspired a best-selling novel by Tony Hillerman, an episode of *Unsolved Mysteries,* and a reenactment on *America's Most Wanted.* This was serious business: a hunt for ruthless cop-killers, antigovernment terrorists who wouldn't hesitate to shoot anyone in a uniform, even if it was the benign green and gray of the National Park Service. And it ended as mysteriously as it had begun viciously.

At about 11:30 in the morning of May 28, 1998, three heavily armed and camouflage-clad men stole a water truck from an oil field service area near Ignacio, Colorado. Speculation has been that the three men—Jason McVean, Robert Mason, and Alan "Monte" Pilon—had intended to use the water truck in an Oklahoma City–style bombing of some government facility. Mason and McVean, both from Durango, Colorado, had police records; all three men were known to hold radical, antigovernment political views. Pilon, from nearby Dove Creek, was a declared racist who owed money to the IRS. All three had once been members of a "patriot" group, but were thrown out for their violent views. Among their personal items discovered later were tactical plans for the implementation of chemical warfare, maps, and information on bombs, guns, grenades, and ammunition. Also discovered were lists of huge stores of food, indicating that the three survivalists expected to be on the run for a long, long, time.

The truck was reported to the authorities as stolen but was not seen again until nearly 9:30 the following morning on the east side of Cortez, Colorado, some eighty miles from Ignacio, when police officer Dale Claxton signaled for it to pull over. Before he could get out of his squad car, one of the three men in the truck (it was never determined which one) unleashed a hail of 7.62 x 39 bullets into the door of the cruiser from an automatic weapon, killing Claxton instantly. The truck then proceeded into Cortez with other police in chase, gunmen in the truck shooting at the officers from the truck's windows. "All of a sudden, police cars and sirens were going crazy, and we heard shooting," according to the manager of the M&M Family Restaurants and Truck Stop in Cortez. "This truck went by, and the three occupants were firing shots at five or six police cars behind them."

The cop-killing and subsequent pursuit by authorities paralyzed

The ruins of Hovenweep National Monument yield to the pinon and juniper landscape of the Four Corners area, the last stand for three fugitives in June 1998. (National Park Service, Hovenweep National Monument)

the Cortez area. As reported by the *Denver Post* the following morning, Cortez was in the middle of its busy tourist season, it being the hub city for many of the famous archaeological sites of the Four Corners area. Schools were locked down (ironically, it was the last day of the academic year), nearby Hovenweep National Monument was evacuated and closed, businesses in the small community of Pleasant View were asked to close their doors, and "farmers were told to stop their field work and stay inside." As a small fleet of airplanes and helicopters circled overhead, ranchers armed themselves, while the locked-down students in Pleasant View ate pizza and watched movies.

Before anyone could catch up with them, the three suspects had abandoned the water truck and seized at gunpoint a flatbed truck from a Cortez building contractor. Transforming the truck into an assault vehicle, two of the men rode in the cab while the third straddled the truck's bed with an automatic weapon. Looking for a water truck, Montezuma County sheriff's deputy Jason Bishop drove right past them. The flatbed pulled out behind the cruiser with absolutely no pretense of escape: the gunner on the bed opened fire on the police cruiser, wounding Bishop in the head, rendering him unconscious, and causing him to crash. McVean, Mason, and Pilon probably presumed that Bishop was dead. But they were wrong.

As the suspects rounded a bend onto Montezuma County Road 25, a Colorado State Patrol vehicle approached them, and the suspects fired. Patrolman Steve Keller's cruiser was immediately put out of action when the rain of bullets shattered windows and blew out a tire. Miraculously, a car driven by Cortez police sergeant Sue Betts was riddled by fire from the flatbed but was not disabled and she was not injured. Farther down Road 25, Deputy Todd Martin had decided he had seen enough: he pulled into a church parking lot and got out of his patrol car, hoisting his shotgun. Before Martin could get off a shot, though, fire erupted from the truck's window as well as from whoever was shooting from the flatbed. He was immediately hit in the elbow and knee and disabled. Two other officers, Jim Bob Wynes from Cortez and state trooper Keller, came to Martin's aid. While Wynes tended to Martin's wounds, Keller pursued the shooters in Wynes's cruiser.

Cruisers manned by Montezuma County sheriff officers Lendel

Lawrence, Terry Steele, and Joey Chavez came upon the truck at the intersection of Road 25 and Road G and immediately drew fire. Fortunately, though the cruisers were riddled with automatic gunfire, none of the officers were hit. (In the short time that Bishop and Keller had been wounded and the fusillade at the intersection of Roads 25 and G, it is estimated that as many as five hundred rounds of ammunition had been fired from the truck, "a level of firepower normally found in only the most intense actions," according to one account.) As the truck proceeded at high speed down Road G and crossed the U.S. Highway 160 intersection, more shots rang out, this time hitting a Dumpster and a civilian car. With four cruisers in pursuit and several alarmed drivers looking for cover, the killers took advantage of the confusion to elude the police. The sheriff's officers were not only uncertain about which direction the truck had gone, they were not even sure that all of the fugitives were still in the truck.

Hovenweep National Monument superintendent Art Hutchinson had been following the chase on his police scanner and knew the fugitives might be headed his way. (Hovenweep straddles the Utah–Colorado border west of Cortez and protects six prehistoric, Puebloan-era structures.) Indeed, as Hutchinson drove out to close the entrance gate and warn visitors of the danger, the flatbed approached him and unleashed a hail of gunfire. Although only two bullets hit his vehicle and Hutchinson escaped unscathed, the encounter caused Hutchinson to swerve off the road. Avoiding road blocks set up on major roads and highways, the fugitives then took to country roads and disappeared into Utah's San Juan County via an area known as Cross Canyon.

At some point, the fugitives decided to abandon the truck and continue their escape on foot, leaving behind two SKS assault rifles and three thousand rounds of ammunition. Disturbingly, only two sets of tracks led away from the flatbed, and these disappeared into a nearby creek bottom. After the truck and human tracks were discovered in Cross Canyon, law enforcement officials took up the search with three dog teams. By this time, police from Colorado, Arizona, New Mexico, Utah, and the Navajo Nation had set up an impromptu command center in a school bus in Cross Canyon.

From there the trail went cold for a time. As one newspaper

speculated, "The suspects may have taken a lesson from the Anasazi of old, who apparently thought that the remote canyon country near Hovenweep would provide protection. So far, the numerous side canyons, arroyos, and pockets have shielded the suspects from the massive search effort." Archaeologist, author, and guide for Far Out Expeditions in Cortez, Fred Blackburn, told the *Denver Post* that the fugitives had "more than enough assets out there as long as they want to." With just a few simple snares, Blackburn asserted, anyone could live off the desert's abundant birds, lizards, rabbits, and even big game. A homeopathic tea could be made from the bark of a willow tree. The ubiquitous Prickly Pear cactus could offer a variety of nutritional options, from its fruit (which is said to taste like strawberries) to its meat, which can be fried after its needles have been burned off. Minnows and crawdads can be found in abundance in streambeds. But the most important asset of the area where the suspects chose to flee was the cover the area provided. According to Blackburn, "They could be out on a flat under pinon or juniper trees and nobody could see them." In short, it was a good place to go missing.

With killers on the loose and local law enforcement seemingly outgunned at every turn, late in the day on May 29 Colorado governor Roy Romer mobilized a portion of the National Guard, including three helicopters. "It's one of those terrible things," Romer said. "All we can do is give them the best support, and air support is what they wanted." Within twenty-four hours the National Guard units were reinforced by searchers from more than fifty law enforcement agencies (including agents from the FBI), and eighteen military helicopters, some with sophisticated, infrared tracking equipment. All told, five hundred people were engaged in the search. Naturally, the media also descended on the area in numbers nearly equal to that of the search team. Indeed, one newspaper reported that "media control became a challenge for law enforcement officials, as reporters commandeered helicopters and planes and scanned cellular phone conversations, intent on thoroughly covering the incident." The *CBS Evening News* on May 30 had even led its broadcast with a report on the manhunt.

As the search continued over the Four Corners area—the unique intersection of Utah, Colorado, New Mexico, and Arizona boundaries along the 37th parallel—authorities started to learn more about who they were dealing with. On the night of May 29, the Denver office of the FBI received an anonymous tip that one of the fugitives might be Alan Pilon of Dove Creek, Colorado, and that "he was going to do something drastic." The next day, the Cortez police dispatch center received a call from Robert Mason's parents, concerned because their son had told them he intended to "go camping" with Jason McVean near Cross Canyon. Furthermore, shell casings found at the scene of Dale Claxton's murder matched those of an automatic rifle believed to belong to McVean. Gradually, acquaintances of the three killers came forward to tell the police what they knew: that Pilon, Mason, and McVean had allegedly stored food, clothing, and guns in various places "in preparation for the end of the world, which will be in the year 2000." Pilon announced to people on May 28 that his job site had been moved and that he would be away for a couple of weeks. His family described him as "depressed" over the fact that the IRS was pursuing him for $1,400 in back taxes. Mason's parents described him as a "loner" and "survivalist." Mason's truck—as well as a trailer owned by Pilon—was found at a business owned by McVean's father, fully stocked with camping gear. All this information merely confirmed what law enforcement officials already knew: the three men were armed, desperate, and dangerous.

For four days it appeared that Pilon, Mason, and McVean had disappeared without a trace. Then on June 4, Robert Mason was spotted by a social worker on lunch break at a picnic area near Swinging Bridge, which spans the San Juan River just east of Bluff, Utah. This was roughly forty-two miles from where the truck had been abandoned. Mason fired upon the social worker, Stephen Wilcox, but missed. Wilcox quickly scrambled to his car, drove away from the area, and called 911. San Juan County Deputy Sheriff Kelly Bradford was in the vicinity and responded immediately. Emerging from his police cruiser on a small rise above the picnic area, Bradford was fired upon by Mason and struck by two bullets. As search teams arrived and started sweeps of the area, Bradford was pulled away to safety. Although alive, his wounds were described as "serious." In the meantime, search teams closed in on Mason, eventually surrounding him. Trapped, Mason took his own life. When

Police officers from the Navajo Nation joined members of the Colorado and Utah state patrols, FBI, and Colorado National Guard in a search for the killers, which ultimately involved five hundred armed men and women and eighteen helicopters (photo by Carol Whitaker; reprinted with permission)

searchers reached his body they also found several pipe bombs; fearing that his body might be booby-trapped—they later determined it wasn't—they arranged for a winch to move it the following morning. Fearing that the other two fugitives were in the area, the authorities called for the evacuation of Bluff and set up an impromptu refugee camp at Albert R. Lyman Middle School in Blanding, Utah, twenty miles to the north.

An unwitting witness to and captive of all this activity was Denver artist Carol Whitaker, who had been poking around the region in her VW camper looking at real estate. On June 3 she left Cortez and literally traced the fugitives' escape route, though she avoided areas that were obviously cordoned off by the police. She found McElmo Canyon "calm and quiet," without "a sign of the prior week's police chase." She felt confident enough to visit a property just behind Ismay's Trading Post (about halfway between Cortez and Bluff), but when she saw an Ismay brother with a shotgun in the front window, she wisely decided not to stop, thinking that if "an Ismay brother was still worried, I certainly should be." She proceeded directly to Bluff without stopping. Along the way it crossed her mind that the fugitives might try to hijack her camper, and that her only defense was a can of pepper spray and a cell phone—"a mere tease compared to an AK-47." She comforted herself in the fact that her VW camper could only make 45 miles per hour uphill, making it hardly a desirable escape vehicle.

Carol had expected to camp in the town of Bluff on private land that was available for purchase from a local Realtor, but once she got there she discovered the road to the property had been torn up for a new water line. She was unable to find the Realtor but left a message with some friends that she would find him in the morning. She then proceeded out of town and found a campsite at Sand Island along the San Juan River, about four miles from Bluff. Finding a site shielded from view by tamarisk and a large cottonwood tree, she cautiously left the rear hatch open for fresh air. Although she knew the three dangerous fugitives were still at large, logic dictated they would have fled south, perhaps into Mexico, to make their escape. Little did she know, at least one of the men was less than two miles away.

At midnight she woke to a sound that "echoed like a shotgun blast." Warily peering out her van's windows, she saw nothing in the moonlit campsite. Suddenly, she recalled, "I realized my foolish imagination had taken over. The sound was not a shotgun blast. Instead, the wind had slammed the hatchback on my van." At dawn she was again awakened by "someone or something" moving around outside her van, but it turned out to be a skunk scratching around a fire pit. An hour later, a car drove through the campground, driving "dangerously close" to her van. The car stopped, and "a tall man, large in girth, wearing jeans and menacing hiking boots, climbed out and stomped in my direction." Carol rooted around for her pepper spray, which was now hopelessly lost somewhere in her sleeping bag. The man approached the windshield and peered inside at Carol, who was dressed only in a long T-shirt but still half stuffed in her sleeping bag. "Carol?" he abruptly asked. At that moment, she realized the stranger was the Realtor she had been trying to find, and he had been looking for her. After three false alarms, she rose, dressed, and drove into town for breakfast with him.

After spending the morning touring properties in Bluff, the Realtor suggested they drive twenty miles up the road to Blanding to meet a friend of his and see her house. Carol agreed to the short trip, thinking she would leave Bluff that afternoon and head home to Denver. In a decision she would later regret, she left her van in Bluff and drove to Blanding in the Realtor's car. As they were about halfway up the road that leads out of the Bluff Valley, a police car came "flying over the hill," lights on and siren blaring. A few minutes later, another police cruiser passed them, then two more, then an ambulance. Realizing this was too much of a response for a simple accident, Carol concluded that it "could only be for the cop-killers. . . . I desperately wanted to turn around and go back."

But the Realtor was unfazed and insisted on proceeding to Blanding to see his friend's house, which sat above the town with a spectacular view of the valley. "Almost the instant we walked in," Carol recalled, "we witnessed the Blackhawk helicopters begin the procession from Cortez across the valley and descend into Bluff." Within thirty minutes they had received a phone call delivering the news that Kelly Bradford had been shot and that Bluff had been evacuated. Even more disturbing to Carol was the news that a woman had been shot at while picnicking at the Sand Island campground that afternoon. All of a sudden Carol "felt vulnerable, stranded in Blanding, dependent on strangers in Blanding for transportation, and frightened that I could have been the woman shot at Sand Island." She insisted that the Realtor drive her to the police station in Blanding, to "get the facts, and see when we could go back to Bluff to get my vehicle, hoping to escape as quickly as possible back to Denver and the security of my well-alarmed home."

As it turns out, there was no need to go to the police station, because the police and other law enforcement officials were everywhere to be seen in Blanding. Activity in the town froze as people listened to police scanners or watched the helicopters circle in the afternoon sky. Resigned to having to spend the night in Blanding, at about 3 p.m. Carol started inquiring about a hotel room. "For the following forty-eight hours," she recalled, "my freedom became limited because of three paramilitary wackos. I was indirectly held hostage." She inquired at the local Super 8 motel, which tried to turn her away after the FBI and Utah Highway Patrol booked forty rooms. Playing the vulnerable woman card (which she was) and pointing out that all she possessed were the clothes she was currently wearing, she talked herself into a room. Fortunately, she had her purse with plenty of cash and credit cards to purchase such essentials as a tooth brush. However, she had left behind her "survival kit," which, "in the future might also contain a police scanner, infrared binoculars, and a clean pair of socks."

Her mood improved once a night's lodging had been secured:

> I began to relax. We also began to have rumors verified.
> The first shooting was not at a woman picnicking. It was
> instead at a welfare worker wearing a uniform and driv
> ing a state car, so fear of random shootings of individuals
> dissipated. The shooting had also not been at Sand Is
> land, my campsite. Instead it was . . . upriver. Calming
> down, I was also comforted that I would be staying at
> a hotel heavily gunned by the various law enforcement
> agencies. What safer place could I be in?

Things were not so great in Bluff, however:

> The news . . . was grim. Bluff had been completely evac
> uated and over 500 law enforcement officers had descended
> on the town. Listening to police scanners in Blanding,
> one learned that various forces were being assembled from
> all over the state . . . word came from CNN that one of
> the three criminals had been found dead, apparently by
> suicide, and wired with multiple pipe bombs.

Still, Carol rested that night with the comfort that she was surrounded by roughly a hundred well-armed FBI agents and officers of the Utah State Patrol. When she rose the following morning, it occurred to her that she was "the only single woman in a motel with over a hundred physically fit men, and I had no makeup, no change of clothes, and no perfume. My luck." She spent the day touring Blanding's few museums and hiking in the nearby hills. After being advised that Bluff would remain evacuated for at least one more day, she booked another night at the motel. She was finally able to talk her way into Bluff the following day and returned to

Denver shortly thereafter. "The manhunt of the century seemed a distant time and a distant place," she recalled, "but I doubt I'll be camping alone again in the Four Corners area anytime soon."

By June 8, admitting they had not the "slightest idea" where McVean and Pilon were, officials drastically scaled back what was called "the greatest Western manhunt in recent memory." Search teams would no longer be airlifted to remote areas, the bulk of the patrol work to be turned over to the sheriffs of Dolores and Montezuma counties in Colorado and San Juan County in Utah. Still, National Guard units remained on standby to fill in for the exhausted local law enforcement officials if need be. "We all feel like zombies," said a sheriff deputy of Montezuma County, Bob Johnson. "The scary thing is that any cop who runs into them (the fugitives) today, tomorrow, or any time in the future is in danger." By June 16 law enforcement officials had further cut back on the manhunt, shifting the emphasis from searches to intelligence gathering.

Then on June 30, authorities caught a break when reports of a "credible sighting" of Pilon and McVean prompted a resumption of the manhunt. A nine-year-old Navajo girl had seen two camouflage-clad men snooping around her uncle's water truck in Montezuma Creek, Utah, and had provided detailed descriptions to law enforcement officials. (Among the details the girl provided was that one of the men walked with a limp. Pilon had been in a motorcycle accident the preceding winter, and was known to have a limp.) For all the force brought to bear in the area following the killing of Dale Claxton on May 29, the sighting occurred within eight miles of Bluff, whose residents had been reporting such oddities as unexplained tracks and stolen food since June 4. The Navajo girl's discovery had confirmed that the fugitives had completely eluded one of the largest manhunts in the history of the West.

Another possible sighting was made the following day, when Navajo police heard two men laughing and splashing around in the San Juan River. Not wishing to risk an ambush and without functioning night-vision equipment, the officers didn't pursue the men, though they were reasonably certain they were Pilon and McVean. "How many people would be out frolicking in the river at two thirty in the morning?" San Juan County sheriff Mike Lacy said in response to a reporter's question as to the veracity of the sighting.

If the two men spotted in the river were indeed McVean and Pilon, then that was the last time anyone had seen them alive. Seventeen months later on October 3, 1999, eleven Navajo deer hunters came across Monte Pilon's skeleton under a juniper tree less than a mile and a half from where the fugitives had abandoned the flat bed truck. The discovery of Pilon's remains only added to the mystery of the manhunt: though coroners could not specifically say what killed Pilon, it is most likely he was killed by a gunshot wound to the head. Whether he committed suicide or was shot by McVean or Mason will never be known. Pilon also had a broken ankle, which might also explain why only two sets of footprints could be found leading away from the flatbed truck. And his body was found in a spot that commanded views of several nearby roads. Indeed, search teams had walked right by the juniper tree numerous times when the manhunt was at its height.

A plausible scenario is that Pilon had broken his ankle early in the chase, and, now a liability to the remaining two fugitives, either Mason or McVean had shot him and stashed his body under the juniper. Still, this does not explain the sighting of two men a month following Mason's suicide. Given the inability of the coroner to establish the precise time of Pilon's death, Pilon might have died or been killed by McVean some time after the manhunt had been called off. We'll never know.

For a time, it seemed the fate of Jason McVean would remain unknown, too. As retired professor of psychology and freelance writer Hal Mansfield had reported in *Crime Magazine*, various theories about McVean's whereabouts circulated—that he had fled the area immediately; that he stayed in the area during the "intense phases" of the manhunt, receiving support from a person or people on the outside; or that he had died.

Robert Mason's parents and Jason McVean's father and stepmother made a public apology to all the victims of their sons' mayhem in the May 20, 2000, issue of the *Denver Post*. Officer Jason Bishop, who had been shot in the back of the head in pursuit of the flatbed truck, recovered and ultimately left police work. Officers Todd Martin and Kelly Bradford also recovered from their wounds, Martin later joining the Colorado State Patrol and Bradford remaining with the San Juan County Sheriff's Department.

The spectre of a still-at-large Jason McVean haunted the Four Corners area for nine years. A $162,500 reward for finding McVean—dead or alive—was posted, and was still in effect when on June 5, 2007, a sixty-one-year-old cowboy came across what he thought was a buried saddle blanket in Cross Canyon, about two and a half miles from where Pilon's remains had been discovered by the Navajo hunters in 1999. The saddle blanket turned out to be a bulletproof vest, and investigators later discovered bones, a fractured skull, an AK-47 assault rifle, and a backpack containing pipe bombs all in the vicinity of the vest. Authorities were "ninety-nine percent sure" the remains were McVean's. "I always figured he was dead the whole time," said San Juan, Utah, county sheriff Mike Lacy, "but until you find him, you never know."

Ironically, Dale Claxton's son Corbin, who was eleven years old at the time of his father's murder at the hands of three vigilantes, had joined the Cortez Police Department just three weeks before the discovery of McVean's remains. "It's good to have him here," said Cortez police chief Roy Lane. "He has a lot of his dad's characteristics."

III

SNOWBOUND

F or all the scenic beauty and economic benefit it provides, winter is by far the American West's deadliest season, whether on the roads, on the slopes, in the backcountry, or even in the front yard. Although the same can probably be said of the continent as a whole, the climate and topography of the West can conspire to make weather unusually swift and severe. It is no surprise, for example, that the greatest temperature drop ever recorded for a twenty-four-hour period occurred on the lee side of the Rockies in Browning, Montana, on January 23–24, 1916. Browning, the site of the Blackfeet Indian Reservation just east of Glacier National Park, was enjoying warm, downslope winds that pushed the temperature up to 56°F one day, only to have the passage of an arctic front drop the temperature to a frigid 7°F the following day. Anyone who has lived in the West through more than one winter is familiar with the pattern of "the warm before the storm"; an approaching front pushes winds downslope, creating friction and warming the atmosphere. After passage of the front winds shift eastward, creating an upslope flow that cools the atmosphere and often produces precipitation in the form of snow. Though tired to the point of being annoying, the expression "If you don't like the weather, just wait five minutes" must have been coined by some early observer of the West's quirky weather. Taken another way, it serves as an admonishment to any outdoorsman who succumbs to the complacency of a Chinook.

And then there is snow. Though most of the West is known as

a dry region, the Lower Forty-Eight's record snow totals can all be found west of the Mississippi. The record for the greatest daily snowfall belongs to Georgetown, Colorado, when on December 4, 1913, 63 inches were recorded. Tamarack, California, holds the record for a monthly snowfall with 313 inches of "Sierra Cement" throughout March of 1907. Rainier Paradise Ranger Station in Washington not only has the record for the greatest daily snow depth of 293 inches on April 12, 1974, but also the greatest July–August snowfall total of nearly 100 feet from August 1973 to July 1974. Though the Rainier record occurred in a part of the West most favorable to precipitation, the Pacific Northwest, that it represents roughly 11 feet of water ranks it right up there with the liquid deposits on a modest rain forest. Finally, any ski area worthy of the name in the West will average between 200 and 300 inches at its summit; add to that the spring storms that might dump 2 to 3 feet on a city like Denver or Salt Lake City, and it's easy to see how life can be simultaneously enriched and disrupted by snowfall. And in the high country of the West, it can snow during any month of the year—although to natives the first snow of the season, usually occurring around the autumnal equinox, is the true harbinger of winter, where coats are retrieved from closets and cars are sent to the shop to have studs shot into their tires.

Winter weather in the West can have a crippling and occasionally deadly impact on aviation, which is more fully explored later. Needless to say, driving conditions also deteriorate rapidly as snow falls and ice forms; most drivers become unwitting captives of the elements, notwithstanding the growing accuracy of forecasts and the increasingly ubiquitous presence of all-wheel-drive vehicles. However, those who have placed themselves most in danger in winter have not been the airline passenger or the interstate driver, but the out-of-bounds or backcountry skier or snowboarder. Statistics clearly bear this out, and notwithstanding warnings and campaigns to raise awareness, the number of avalanche and backcountry fatalities has doubled in the past twenty years.

There are two basic ways you can die in the backcountry in winter: get lost, run out of provisions, and freeze to death; or succumb to an avalanche. Since 1984, 416 people have died in the continental United States from avalanches; all but nine of these deaths occurred west of the Mississippi (New Hampshire and New York, seven and two fatalities, respectively). Being a significant destination point for skiers and 'boarders, and also comprising a resident population known to be one of the most outdoors-oriented in the country, the state of Colorado leads the nation in avalanche fatalities at about six a year for the past twenty years. Even populous California trails Colorado by a wide margin; furthermore, Utah, Washington, and Wyoming have each recorded more avalanche fatalities annually than the Golden State since 1985.

Who are the victims? The Colorado Avalanche Information Center, a repository for U.S. avalanche data, breaks fatalities down by "activity," and to the surprise of no one backcountry and out-of-bounds skiers and boarders have accounted for more than 25 percent of all such deaths over the past two decades. Snowmobilers comprise the next largest group of avalanche victims, followed by climbers. Only a handful of what one would call "innocent bystanders" have been killed in avalanches since 1985—the unlucky motorist or highway worker, even an inbounds skier in the winter of 2005. And the profile of a typical avalanche victim is of a white male between the ages of twenty and twenty-nine, certainly a statement on the power of testosterone.

Although avalanches can occur at any time of year and on any slope given favorable conditions, the avalanche "season" in the West runs from January through June, according to the frequency of recorded fatalities. An avalanche can occur on slopes facing any direction and with as little as a ten-degree slope angle, but most occur on slopes that face north, east, or northeast at a slope angle between thirty and forty-five degrees. The most common type of avalanche is the "slab" avalanche, where a layer of snow will disengage from a slope's surface (usually another layer of ice or snow) and barrel downhill, taking with it debris in the form of rocks and trees. Analogous to snow sliding off a car's rear window as the defroster heats up, many slab avalanches occur as the weather warms up following a heavy snowfall.

According to a website on avalanche awareness maintained by the National Snow and Ice Data Center (NSIDC) at the University of Colorado, the easiest way to avoid an avalanche is to simply stay out of the backcountry during winter. However, realizing this will

hardly deter the adventurer or thrill-seeker (see avalanche victim profile, above), the NSIDC recommends that anyone in the backcountry
carry a shovel, collapsible probe or ski-pole probe, and avalanche
beacon. If caught in an avalanche, NSIDC further advises the following:

> Yell and let go of ski poles and get out of your pack to
> make yourself lighter. Use "swimming" motions, thrust-
> ing upward to try to stay near the surface of the snow.
> When avalanches come to a stop and debris begins to
> pile up, the snow can set as hard as cement. Unless you
> are on the surface and your hands are free, it is almost
> impossible to dig yourself out. If you are fortunate enough
> to end up near the surface (or at least know which di-
> rection it is), try to stick out an arm or a leg so that res-
> cuers can find you quickly.
>
> If you are in over your head (not near the surface),
> try to maintain an air pocket in front of your face using
> your hands and arms, punching into the snow. When an
> avalanche finally stops, you will have from one to three
> seconds before the snow sets. Many avalanche deaths are
> caused by suffocation, so creating an air space is one of
> the most critical things you can do. Also, take a deep
> breath to expand your chest and hold it; otherwise, you
> may not be able to breathe after the snow sets. To pre-
> serve air space, yell or make noise only when rescuers are
> near you. Snow is such a good insulator they probably
> will not hear you until they are practically on top of you.
>
> Above all, do not panic. Keeping your breathing steady
> will help preserve your air space and extend your sur-
> vival chances. If you remain calm, your body will be bet-
> ter able to conserve energy.

Most survivors dig themselves out or are dug out within fifteen
to thirty minutes of being trapped. Victims buried longer than forty-
five minutes "rarely survive."

Several of the accounts that follow are drawn from the Colorado
Avalanche Information Center's comprehensive log of accidents through-

out the United States from 1996 to 2007. Although far too many of these accounts can be tragically summarized simply as "caught, buried, killed," a few stand out as cautionary tales that illustrate the sheer capriciousness of avalanches. Others demonstrate that all the precautions in the world won't stop a determined backcountry skier, boarder, or sledder. Finally, we've included a number of avalanche survivor stories, since seldom do avalanche victims get to tell us what it's really like to be buried in a snowslide.

A Yellowstone Avalanche

Avalanche fatalities in our oldest national park are rare, mostly because backcountry skiers and snowmobilers tend to stick to established roads and trails. For Yellowstone's dedicated scientists, however, backcountry research is a year-round proposition, notwithstanding the risk. On March 3, 1997, one of the park's leading and most popular scientists was taken by an avalanche. The official park press release describing the accident follows.

YELLOWSTONE NATIONAL PARK EMPLOYEE DIES IN ACCIDENT

Yellowstone National Park officials report that Research Geologist, Roderick (Rick) A. Hutchinson has been killed in an avalanche in the Heart Lake area in south-central Yellowstone National Park. A visiting seismic geologist, whose name is being withheld pending notification of relatives and who was also suspected to be caught in the avalanche, has not yet been found.

Hutchinson and the visiting geologist traveled to Heart Lake patrol cabin over the weekend where they monitored thermal features in the area. The trail to Heart Lake is about 8 miles long, starting from the South Entrance Road a few miles south of Grant Village. Hutchinson had communicated by radio with park rangers at approxi-

mately 8 a.m. on Monday, March 3, arranging to meet rangers half-way between Heart Lake and the trailhead on Tuesday afternoon. When park rangers traveled to the area late Tuesday afternoon, they failed to meet up with Hutchinson and the visiting geologist. They observed several avalanches at the base of Factory Hill (near Mt. Sheridan), and continued on to the cabin, where they discovered the personal belongings of Hutchinson and his companion. The park rangers then returned to the avalanche site (around 9 p.m.) and observed ski tracks going in and out of the first avalanche, and entering but not exiting the second avalanche. By this time, the weather was deteriorating and the decision was made to continue a wider search at first light.

On Wednesday morning, the search was resumed. However, dangerous avalanche conditions prevented access to the site where the last ski tracks were observed. Experts were brought in to use explosives to help decrease the danger of additional avalanches. Four search dog teams were brought in to begin a search of the avalanche debris area. Probe teams began their work on early Wednesday afternoon. The search was halted at dark and continued again at first light on Thursday morning.

At 4:30 p.m., Thursday, searchers discovered a ski pole belonging to Hutchinson and shortly after, discovered his body. Rick had apparently been skiing westbound along the flank of Factory Hill. He was not headed for the trail, but was using his normal route up Witch Creek to visit a thermal feature. He was found in no more than 4 feet of snow by a probe line. Dogs were not in use at the time. The search for the visiting seismic geologist is continuing.

Rick Hutchinson began working for the National Park Service in Yellowstone as a Seasonal Interpretive Specialist in 1970. He received a Career-Conditional Appointment as a Geothermal Specialist in 1973 and was promoted to Geologist in 1976. He was known by scientists throughout the world for his deep familiarity with Yellowstone's geothermal resources, and was the author of many publications, reports, and papers on the park's unique geological wonders. His wife, Jennifer J. Whipple, is also an employee of the park.

Superintendent Michael Finley expressed his deep sorrow at Rick's death. Speaking on behalf of the entire Yellowstone staff, Finley stated, "For more than a quarter of a century, Rick Hutchinson has been a Yellowstone institution, one of those rare, authentic experts who can be counted on to help the many people, visitors and researchers alike, who come and go in a place like Yellowstone. It was almost as if he was a part of the park itself, a gentle presence that had always been here and would go on forever. Nobody loved Yellowstone more, or was more wholly devoted to embracing its spirit and caring for its wonders. Rick touched many lives here, and will not be forgotten."

Killed in Their Sleep

The unpredictability of avalanches was no better demonstrated than in a slide that occurred east of Logan, Utah, during the night of January 11, 1997, when three experienced campers were swept to their deaths on a southwest-facing slope above Logan Canyon known as "the folly." Notwithstanding its moniker, the area was not known for avalanches, which is probably why the backcountry skiers chose to camp there.

According to Mike Jenkins of the Utah Avalanche Forecast Center, a "perfect storm" of weather conditions had come together to produce the slide, and he had even upgraded his own advisory on the day of the incident after new snow had fallen on a "rain crust" covering old snow. Jenkins hypothesized that a "hard slab" formed by intense northwest winds had broken loose at about nine thousand feet and had run about one thousand feet down the thirty-five-degree slope.

The campers' bodies were not discovered until a search-and-rescue team was dispatched after the campers failed to return home at the scheduled time. It wasn't until 9:00 p.m. on January 13 that ten backcountry skiers and a rescue dog were sent out to look for them, but thanks to a tip from a party that had seen the campers early on January 11, the rescue team was able to locate the debris field by 10:30 p.m. Moreover, one of the victim's transceivers had been activated and was still working, enabling a beacon search to locate the bodies. Jenkins described the "burial site" as being "150 feet above the toe of the slide in thick timber."

Rescuers used probes to locate the campers' bodies, but the com-pacted snow—between four and six feet deep—was hard to clear, and the bodies were not completely uncovered until midnight. Ac-cording to Jenkins, "All three victims were in their sleeping bags in their tent which was wrapped around a tree." The cause of death was determined to be suffocation. The victims were well known in the local community and experienced outdoor enthusiasts. Jenkins re-marked that in two decades of skiing in the area he had never seen an avalanche of this magnitude, and that the area was not generally known as dangerous.

A Warm-Weather Avalanche

It wasn't quite summer, but it might as well have been because high temperatures led to dangerous snowpack conditions on the slopes of Washington's Mount Rainier in the late spring of 1998. These conditions prompted a particularly insidious snowslide that struck two climbing teams on June 11, proving that avalanches can occur anytime of year given the right (or wrong) conditions. It was the first known avalanche in the part of the mountain known as Disappointment Cleaver in more than twenty years, but it might not have taken very much to trigger it.

Described as "wet and frighteningly fast," the avalanche tumbled down on as many as ten climbers roped together in two teams above the 11,000-foot level of the mountain. The first report, from another climbing party equipped with a cell phone 400 feet above the slide, was that they may have all been killed. As it happens, a search-and-rescue ranger, Mike Gauthier, overheard the emergency call while on Rainier's summit. He immediately strapped on his snowboard, descended 3,000 feet, and was at the scene of the slide within twenty-six minutes. As recounted by Butch Farabee in his book *Death, Daring, and Disaster: Search and Rescue in the National Parks*, Gauthier was

> . . . able to make an immediate size-up for those already gearing up below . . . two separate groups with up to 10 climbers, were missing. The scene was extremely hazardous

An avalanche can occur at any time of the year on Washington's Mount Rainer.
(National Park Service, Mount Rainier National Park)

with 40-degree icy slopes, 20-foot vertical rock bands, exposure to more avalanches, and then a 300 foot drop to the glacier below.

One group of climbers was dangling off a refrigerator-sized rotten rock; the other clung to a cliff or dangled on a rope which was dangerously frayed down to its inner strands and pulled tight over a sharp rock held by just one anchor. Patrick Nestler, a 29-year-old client, had fallen substantially farther than the others and was below the rest of his group.

The National Park Service assembled a small army of rangers, Mountain Rescue Association volunteers, local guides, and two helicopters and swept into action. As Farabee explains:

SAR [Search and Rescue] teams were inserted on to the mountain's steep, ice-covered slopes with both Army and private helicopters. Some of the rescuers climbed to the accident site to assist with the raising evacuation while other teams headed to the base of the cleaver to assist with the lowering of Nestler. Rescuers negotiated the cliff [by] securing the injured and triaging the patients. Most victims had combinations of serious hand and leg injuries, as well as three who were already hypothermic. Rescuers were racing the nightfall.

To get Nestler the others on his rope had to be raised first. Then, the best way for him to go was down. As quickly as possible Nestler was lowered off the cliff, taken across the bergschrund and evacuated to the waiting Chinook where he was pronounced dead.

Nestler had died from severe trauma and not the usual cause of death from avalanche, suffocation. Seven of the remaining climbers were taken to local hospitals, but most injuries were reported as minor—a tribute to the quick response of national park rangers and their cadre of volunteers. As Mount Rainier National Park spokeswoman Maria Gillett modestly stated, "We were really fortunate not to have more deaths or more serious injuries."

A Close Call

Unlike the unlucky campers killed in their sleep in Logan Canyon in January 1997, Coloradan Jim Jackson survived the demolition of his cabin by an avalanche near Silverton on March 29, 1998. According to Andy Gleason of the Colorado Avalanche Information Center, the Class 5 avalanche—avalanches are rated on a scale of 1 to 5, with 5 being the most extreme and destructive—swept over the cabin at two in the morning. Jackson, asleep in the top bunk, was first awakened by the sound of shattered glass as snow poured in through the windows. The cascading snow then ripped the roof off a mere six inches above his head. Though Jackson was unhurt, the cabin had been completely destroyed, having survived another avalanche fifteen years earlier. Examination of the avalanche revealed a deep fracture line and a debris field approximately 50 feet high. The avalanche had been so powerful it had run 1,500 feet, crossed a gully, and continued 150 feet *uphill* to smash the cabin.

An "Urban" Avalanche and Its
Wild Victims

Heagle Park in Hailey, Idaho, looks like any other city park with its broad, green lawns, picnic tables, and open-air shelters. In early February 1999, however, Heagle Park became the terminus of an avalanche that took the lives of at least twenty deer (and one rainbow trout). The force of the slide from Della Mountain nearly reached two neighborhoods, though no human fatalities or injuries were reported. One witness to the avalanche had seen a herd of about fifty deer nervously trying to cross a bowl of unstable snow just prior to the slide, "then they all just went down. It was a free-fall to the river about two hundred yards below." Those at the scene saw hooves protruding through the snow.

The avalanche also took its toll on Heagle Park, destroying a picnic shelter, two tables, and a tree. Though there were no reported human injuries, debris reached two neighborhoods in Hailey and dammed the Big Wood River, almost causing flooding in surrounding neighborhoods. It was there that Ray Hyde, head of the Hailey Water and Sewer Department, came across the avalanche's final victim. "I saw one 12-inch rainbow sticking up out of the snow that had an expression that was priceless," he recalled.

Buried Alive

The sheer terror of being caught in an avalanche is captured in the vivid account that follows. It's best told in the victim's own words, a combination of the "hey, dude" patois of the 'boarder and the shock of an experienced backcountry rider (one who has taken all the right precautions) to find himself buried in an area of Mount Rainier not known for avalanches. Though his ordeal lasted only five or six minutes, it is clear from this account that they were the longest five or six minutes of his young life.

9 LIVES—November 24, 2001

This is a backcountry snowboarding story of how I lived to tell you about this backcountry snowboarding story. Usually people who make this many mistakes don't get the chance to tell the story, so here goes.

Yesterday, November 24th, was the first day of the 2001 season for me and I wanted to go backcountry. Baker and Crystal were opening up the 25th, but I didn't want to wait in long lift lines for tracked up rocks and my body needed conditioning that only earned turns can give.

I was going up to camp Muir at about 10,000ft on the S. side of Rainier solo or not. I knew the route well, knew it would be crowded and knew it had very little if any avalanche danger. I sound confident and cocky—I was. The night before my good buddy and touring partner Gorio called me and was in. Between the two of us we've done this tour over 40 times. I brought my compass, transceiver, probe, shovel, first aid/repair kit and enough food and clothes for the trip including an extra night if needed. If I had any concern at all it was of spending an extra night on the mountain, and even that was so faint I consciously didn't bring a map or wands knowing I could dig in and survive.

The trip from door to door is about 12 hours so I told Gorio I'd be at his house at 4am. We were at the Longmire gate at 630am and were told the gate probably would not open until 11am due to snow, though very little snow had fallen overnight. We had breakfast and debated between our options, but with most roads closed in and around Rainier our only option was to drive to Hood and ride there. I guess you could call it a lucky break but the gate opened at about 8am and we were in the Paradise parking lot getting ready to head up shortly after. While packing Gorio told me he had not really slept and forgot his transceiver (mistake #1), no biggy to me, my decision to go on was made without a second thought.

We were first on the mountain and broke trail as the wind and little bit of snow had wiped clean any signs of an up track. We were still in the trees and lower section of the mountain, but the wind was serious even at this elevation (avy clue #1), which meant it would be even more ferocious above tree line. At one point Gorio and I were together when a gust blew both of us 2ft back. Wishing I had a facemask we climbed on.

Our first stop was going to be an old roofless shelter at the top of the steepest section of the climb, about 1500–2000ft from the parking lot and 3000ft from Muir. As we approached the wind was in our face and several times we had to lean to the ground to hang on. We finally had to take our skis off and scramble. Two skiers we met in the parking lot, Jimmy and Sam, had caught up to us in the shelter. We were out of the wind, but without a roof there was a constant swirl of snow in the air. Any pack, glove or exposed hand was instantly covered or filled with snow. We ate and drank hot tea. Gorio and I were still in for going to Muir as Jimmy and Sam decided to head down and ski terrain less windy.

We made it about 200ft from the shelter and ran into some climbers on the way down, they had spent the night in tents at about 8000ft and said it was like camping in the jetstream. I was impressed. My spare pair of socks that I'd tied together around my face was not working, the two knots prevented my jacket from closing completely and they really didn't protect my exposed skin. Pressing on meant no exposed skin, so after about 10 minutes we turned back.

Our first turns were awesome as we were on the leeward side, though the wind had buffeted all sides, this was a deep firm powder that was easy to board. By now we had 20 skiers, climbers and boarders in sight. The firm snow showed no signs of weakness and we did not plan on digging any pits (mistake #2).

Though neither of us had headed SE of the parking lot, we could see the parking lot and snow covered road (closed in winter) heading east out of it. All we had to do was make it back to the road and ski back to the lot. Plus, we could see other skiers touring in all directions, so we were not alone. On the way down Gorio spotted some avalanche debris (avy clue #2), the first we'd seen. After about 1000ft of turns we switched back and headed for more leeward slopes to the east. Gorio spotted a great line that was tucked in next to a top to bottom line of trees; we were at the top an hour later.

After windsurfing with our bodies at the top of the ridge and having lunch we rode down one at a time. I'd say we were still being fairly safe riding one at a time and keeping each other in sight. In retrospect I was all too confident in the snow and my ability to react to anything the mountain could dish out. In fact I remember thinking that very thought only hours before. At the time I thought it I wondered if the mountain could sense my confidence. I would later regret that thought.

We were now in the ride to the bottom with as little hiking as possible mode. As with many of the volcanoes in early or late season this means keeping your board on at all costs (mistake #3). So we were heading SW trying to make as many turns while not losing elevation, maybe even hoping to keep a line that could deposit us back in the parking lot without any more hiking. It's early season and I was pooped.

We were about 500 vertical feet above the parking lot and maybe a 1/2 mile east when we started working the beginnings of a creek. At first it was a wide opening and I made some steep turns just in front of Gorio, nothing moved. We regrouped and looked at the terrain trap below as the creek got narrower and the slopes into it steeper.

I could see a way out across a 100ft wide mini-bowl, nothing that big at all. It was right next to the steep slope I had just come down. I didn't even look up to see what could cut loose on me or look down to really see where I would go if it did (mistake #4). It was a classic avy slope ready to rip and I was too close to safety and too cocky to even see it.

I had just entered it, trying to cut a high line straight across its belly (mistake #5) putting as much pressure as my 230 lbs of body and gear could put on it still only thinking of making the high point 100ft away without hiking.

At the same time Gorio yelled "slide" I saw the snow in front of me start to move. I was only about 5ft in and it looked like only the top 8–12 inches was moving, but for sure a big island of snow. At this point I thought I was still in control and there was no panic. I instantly turned my board back toward the direction I had come and the moving snow forced me to sit though I had hoped to keep moving as I had in many slides before. After about 20ft I realized I was going to get forced into a narrow crux of the creek and I realized this was going to be big. Everything was happening so fast and at the same time *in slow motion, I didn't try to pull my ripcord that releases my board, or take off my pack, both would be anchors and all avy training says to ditch the gear. About this time the secondary wave of snow from above, that had a 2–3ft crown at its deepest point in a 20ft wide section, hit me from behind with speed. This is the last time Gorio saw me as I was buried from this point on. I traveled the next 40+ feet face down thinking I would be going down a long way not really knowing what was around the bend in the creek. I was still calm considering I was buried. I tried to reach my board to pull the rip cord but it was uphill. Before I knew it things were coming to a stop, I just managed to get my right hand in front of my face and my left hand about 10 inches away.*

The first 10 seconds:

Oh my god, Oh my god. Keep calm, everything you've learned says to conserve oxygen and keep calm. I was calm for one second, and shitting my pants the next.

My goggles were still on and I could see, there was light. I tried to move but the snow was cement. My body was stretched out to the fullest, as my board was an anchor with my body and pack being pulled downhill. My head was face down and well below my feet. I knew which way was up. I tried like hell to free myself, to push up, but each time the effort would take up all the oxygen and I felt like I was hyperventilating. Then I tried to yell "Gorio" "Gorio" with the same effect.

I relaxed, regained my breath, and somehow felt calm for just a few seconds.

The next 20 seconds:

I realized Gorio did not have a transceiver . . . did he have his probe??? I knew he had his shovel but how deep was I. I know from experience that avy snow is cement and digging someone out by yourself is compounded many

*times with each foot of snow that is on top of you. But
how the f---! Would he find me without a transceiver???
And if he doesn't have his probe forget it, he has to have
a probe. We're in a hole, no one saw us and there was
not enough time to get help. Fifteen minutes is all I have,
all Gorio has to save me.*

*Is this it? Am I going to die right here? What about
Sara, Reilly and Ivy? F---!! I try to push again and bring
my left hand closer to my face, which fills my little air
pocket and mouth with snow resulting in a double dose
of panic.*

The next 2 minutes:

*All I can think about is my family. Reilly is 2 and Ivy
is 4. How could I miss all the signs and die so early. All
my backcountry experiences, training, first descents and
shit talking and now I'm cemented a half mile from my car.
I'm a f---ing idiot! F---!! They won't find me until next
year, it will just keep snowing and sliding and getting deeper
and deeper.*

*I try to call out to Gorio again, but my breath has
melted the snow, which is now starting to freeze around
my head, greatly reducing the oxygen flow.*

The last 3–4 minutes:

*I've given up hope of being saved 100%. I think my
goggles are starting to fog as it's getting darker and darker.
All I can think about is my wife Sara and kids, the best
kids in the world. I know I'll be hurting them, hurting
the rest of my family and friends. I think how I'm not
going to be able to teach my kids how to love the mountains, and I think they will hate the mountains. I don't
want them to hate the mountains.*

I'm sad, I'm mad, I'm calm then I'm fighting again.

It's dark but I'm still conscious.

I believe in god in my own way, and I ask for his

help. It was weird; it felt like I was asking for my kids and not for me. I felt so sorry for them.

Then I hear it, muffled and about 10 or so feet away.

"Luke" "Luke"

Oh shit, Oh shit. . . . It's Gorio, f---in A it's Gorio. I could only manage one or two "Gorio's," not sure if he heard me or not but just like that with a heart attack of excitement I knew I was going to be dug out.

The next 10 minutes:

It seemed like it only took 10 seconds, could have been a minute I don't know, but Gorio got my face free and I gasped for air screaming "you saved my life, you saved my life." Gorio says I was pretty out of it saying all kinds of shit, all I remember is feeling euphoric and telling Gorio how he saved my life. Gorio was moving fast as we were still in a very dangerous place. It took a minute to dig out my board and get it off my feet when Gorio accidentally knocked some snow in my face blocking my breath. I yelled "Gorio, Gorio my face" as my arms and head were still locked in place. The helplessness was overwhelming.

The strange thing was my goggles were not fogged, I guess the no fog stuff I put on the inside and outside the night before worked and it was my brain that went dark.

I wanted to hug Gorio and Gorio wanted to get the f--- out of Dodge, we had to hike back up the slide path to get out, as below us was an even bigger terrain trap.

My head was pounding from the lack of oxygen, I had no more strength left but the thought of being ripped by another slide and being able to see my family again after giving up hope was more than enough motivation to climb out. Still had one last 20ft section of exposed slope to climb across until we were in a safe zone. Gorio repacked his gear in another safe zone across the creek while I slowly made my way to it even though I was going as fast as I could. Once there I collapsed as I had been climbing the entire time since being set free. Once Gorio made it I went back into my "you saved my life" speech, hugs etc.

Twenty minutes later we were in the parking lot.

I'm still shaking my head. Asking questions. Feeling so happy to be alive, to have a second chance to be with my family. And I can't explain it, but feeling depressed and everything in between.

Gorio said he saw the second wave coming and it hit me hard, he went to a safe spot 20ft away and grabbed his shovel and probe and assembled them both without having to take his moist gloves off, saving time. From the point he last saw me he probed down the narrow creek avy path until he saw a piece of my ski binding on the outside of my pack, the size of a dime, sticking out. The size of a dime! In 5–6 minutes he had my face exposed to air, beautiful air.

His experience was as traumatic as mine; only difference is he had oxygen. He was thinking about how he was going to have to tell Sara about me, how shitty would that have been?

Sara said she wouldn't have been mad at Gorio, it was my decisions that got me into the mess, so she would have been mad at me.

So many times I've cheated death, before my kids I needed to get that rush to feel alive. I'd get it in the mountains, riding bikes, anything to get the rush and feeling invincible. Many times I've paid the price with pain, coming close to the edge and living to tell about it. For the most part I've mellowed out since having kids.

Yesterday I paid the ultimate price, I crossed the line so far I was dead in my own mind.

It's still too close to really know what kind of perspective this will give me, but guaranteed, perspective will be gained.

To my family, Sara, Ivy and Reilly; I love you more than anything. More than solo trips, more than first descents and more than life itself.

To my family and Sara's family who would have had

to deal with the mess, help raise my kids and the entire trauma this would have caused you, I'm sorry.

To Gorio, what can I say or do? For my family and for myself thank you. I'll ask the backcountry community what the going rate is for full body retrieval and life saving while putting yourself at risk. And to you I'm sorry for putting up my blinders.

To anyone who reads this and travels in the backcountry; read the signs, they're out there if you look for them. Take the training, learn from the training and use the training. Always bring your tools; transceiver, probe, shovel and most importantly your brain. This was a teeny tiny slide I was in practically next to the parking lot. I could have been swept down into a creek hole and buried 20ft deep or over a cliff, through rocks or trees and all totally helpless.

I'm not going to stop living life, but I plan on making sure I'm around to enjoy it with my family and friends as long as humanly possible.

I still have a few of those 9 lives left, but I plan on saving the rest for a long, long time.

Loving life,

Luke Edgar

Snowdog

An avalanche survival story of a different kind—what a tale the survivor could tell, if only she could!

On Sunday, April 30, 2000, Jimmy Breitenstein was telemark skiing in the vicinity of Mount Baker ski area with his dog Sketch, and another dog, Champ, which belonged to his friend Gillian Sizemore. He described the weather at the time as "increasing clouds and warming" following two or three days of "moderate to heavy snowfall and strong winds at lowering snow levels." As he was descending and traversing around a cliff band at approximately 4,500 feet, he lost sight of Champ, only to hear a disturbing yelp as a "point release" avalanche of "damp, heavy snow" tumbled over the cliff and ran for "about a hundred and twenty yards to a flat run-out zone." After searching in vain for the dog for two hours, Breitenstein concluded that Champ must have been swept beneath the cliff and then been buried in snow.

Eighteen days later, on Thursday, May 18, ski area employees working with a film crew in a parking lot close to where the avalanche occurred recognized an "emaciated"—yet very much alive—Champ, poking around nearby. They immediately got her to a vet, who noted that she had lost fifteen of her original sixty-five pounds but had not suffered any frostbite. Tellingly, however, her nails were almost completely worn away; it appears that Champ had dug her way out of the snow, perhaps trying for up to two weeks.

As a report on the incident concluded, "Champ, a female German shepherd, is now *the* Champ."

IV

LOST HORIZON: AIR ACCIDENTS

Guidelines for flying in the mountain West read like rules of engagement for combat, except that here the adversaries are atmosphere and topography and the interplay of one with the other. One experienced pilot has noted that Alaska is the most dangerous place to fly within the United States, except, quite notably, "the Rocky Mountains." The list of "don'ts" for mountain and canyon country flying in light aircraft are both onerous and ominous, themselves imagining all sorts of possible calamities unknown to the flatland flyer. Advises one such Internet-based site for mountain flying, mountains are to be avoided if the mountaintop wind speeds exceed 30 knots "unless you are experienced in this type of operation." Routes that don't have emergency landing areas are to be avoided, as well as those that take you down the middle of a canyon. Basically suggesting that pilots throw out all their assumptions about weather when flying in the mountains, it cautions that "air, although invisible, acts like water and it will flow along the contour of mountains and valleys. Don't slow down in a downdraft."

Some of the stern yet seemingly obvious advice given mountain pilots seems to play directly into the old flying joke about clouds: "Stay out of clouds. Reliable sources report that mountains have been known to hide out in them." The most basic rule of thumb seems to be "never fly beyond the point of no return" when attempting to cross a mountain ridge. This advice appears to be a sarcastic admonition, but it is actually a technical expression defined as "a point on the ground of rising terrain where the terrain out-climbs the aircraft. The turn-around point is determined as the point where, if the throttle is reduced to idle, the aircraft can be turned around during a glide without impacting the terrain." Furthermore, a ridge or summit is not to be crossed until you can see a fair chunk of landscape on the other side.

Simple enough? Not quite. Distances can be deceiving when flying over contours of light, shadow, forest, and tundra. I recall an anecdote from an air traffic controller a few years back concerning the pilot of a corporate jet he was guiding into Denver International Airport through the "Thompson Gate," an ATC portal directly over Rocky Mountain National Park. In this particular instance the pilot was convinced he was about to fly into the summit of Longs Peak at 14,200 feet when both his instruments and the controller were telling him otherwise. In a panicked voice he asked for clearance to increase his altitude by 2,000 feet. Denied his request, he began bracing his passengers for the worst. The controller let him sweat a little before hearing him squeak "disregard" as he passed safely 4,000 feet over the mountain's summit.

If it was simply terrain and disorientation that challenged the aviator, then perhaps the record of air accidents in recent times would be halved. But there is also the atmosphere, both static and active, that regularly poses challenges even when it appears to be in its most docile state. On a normal summer day in the mountains of western North America, for example, the sun's warmth will provide something called anabatic lift on the lee side or eastward-facing side of a valley, yanking air downslope on the opposing range. As the sun centers over the valley toward midday, both ranges are subject to what is known as "valley breeze," or upslope winds. (Imagine a U-shaped symbol set in the valley floor.) Finally, nighttime cooling produces a rush of air downslope as cool, dense air seeks its lowest possible point.

Keeping track of all this under normal conditions is daunting enough, but we have been talking about climate and topography and not yet weather. Throw into the mix the turbulence of summer thunderstorms, the blindness of a snow squall, the "icy mix" of a spring storm, Chinooks, boras, and Santa Anas, and you wonder why people would want to fly here at all. Indeed, in the accounts that follow, it is clear that some pilots never should have.

Fallen Angel: The Last Flight of
Jessica Dubroff

For a very brief time in the early spring of 1996, hers was a cause célèbre: an attempt to become the youngest person to fly a plane across the continent. Although the *Guinness Book of World Records* had stopped listing "youngest pilot" records in the interest of discouraging such potentially dangerous stunts, seven-year-old Jessica, largely at the urging of her father Lloyd, still captured the attention of the nation as she departed Half Moon Bay, California, on April 10 for her cross-country flight. Accompanied by Lloyd and her flight instructor, Joe Reid, Jessica was determined to fly to Massachusetts and afterward Washington, D.C., where her triumph would be crowned by offering to take President Clinton up for a ride. Lloyd had even arranged for an ABC News camera to be installed on board the plane.

All this seemed extremely far-fetched for a girl, who, just three years before, had been a squatter with her single mother and two siblings in an abandoned house in Falmouth, Massachusetts, accepting food donations from a local health food store. Although Jessica's mother, Lisa Blair Hathaway, had never married Lloyd Dubroff, he remained the sole source of the children's support. The trouble was that Lloyd had come upon hard times as well; in 1993 his computer consulting firm had failed and he had been evicted from his Palo Alto, California, home. He filed for bankruptcy that year and listed debts of $157,000 against assets of $3,754. Complicating matters further was that Dubroff had married and fathered a child with another woman.

According to a son from a previous marriage, Lloyd's fortunes improved dramatically in 1995, citing work with Pacific Bell, Visa Corporation, and PSW3 Financial Services Corporation. Hathaway and her family had also moved back to the Bay Area so the children could be closer to Lloyd, and it was at this time that Jessica started taking flying lessons at Lloyd's expense. Oddly, Jessica was not enrolled in school because of Lloyd's belief that Jessica's $50-an-hour flying lessons were "less than I'd pay for a private school," and that learning how to fly would teach her math, weather forecasting, geography, and physics. Her mother, a self-described "writer, artist, and healing consultant," seemed to go along with this, telling the *San Francisco Examiner* somewhat propitiously that a child's natural state is "non fear. There's no fear. Fear is not a reality to them."

The idea of Jessica's being the nominal pilot for a cross-country trip seemed to have popped into Lloyd's head as would the notion of going on a Sunday afternoon drive after church. "Out of the blue it occurred to me that Jessica could do this," he is quoted as saying. A few were skeptical of Lloyd's motives, however, among them the Palo Alto landlord to whom he still owed several thousand dollars in back rent. "I don't understand how he could come up with the money to pay for a flight like this [approximately $50,000], unless he was planning to write a book and sell it or something like that," said the owner of the house, Suzanne Cahn. Indeed, money may have been a motive, especially since Hathaway had asked the *Examiner* (in the words of the *Examiner*'s reporters) to "report that the family was seeking financial contributions." Citing the fact that Jessica was a vegetarian, she asked for people to supply suitable food along the route. She also suggested to a friend that she had offered the story to *National Geographic* for an undisclosed sum.

Whether it was specifically because of the possible dangers of the projected 6,660-mile, round-trip flight ahead of them, or part of some broader plan to take care of his two families should anything happen to him, Lloyd had also taken out life insurance on himself totaling $3 million. The four policies were to be split evenly between Lisa Hathaway and his wife, Melinda Dubroff.

The first leg of the trip, departing from the salubrious climate of coastal California on April 10, destination Cheyenne, Wyoming, was routine enough, though flying through the intermountain West in early spring can be as risky as it gets for a light aircraft. Jessica's plane was a Cessna 177B, a single-engine, high-winged aircraft with fixed tricycle landing gear. Its 180-horsepower Lycoming engine could push it to a top cruising speed of 123 knots; the plane was capable of flying as high as 14,600 feet. Branded the "Cardinal," the 177B fit the classic Cessna profile for single-engine aircraft and was well liked by pilots for its roomy cabin and sleek looks. (Although only built from 1970 to 1978, used models in good condition still go for $50,000 to $60,000.)

During the flight from Half Moon Bay to Cheyenne, Floyd had flicked on the ABC camera a few times, at one point asking Jessica what she would do "if the engine quit right now." "I don't know," was her straightforward yet mildly disturbing response. Sitting in the right seat, however, was her flight instructor, Joe Reid, the official Pilot-in-Command (or PIC) for the journey. His expertise would presumably come into play should anything happen. But the camera was trained on Jessica, and in order to claim the record the controls had to be in her hands except in an emergency.

The morning of Thursday, April 11, broke windy and cold in Cheyenne, with a fatigued-looking Jessica performing media interviews as hail and rain pelted the Cessna. (The plan was to execute the round-trip flight in eight consecutive days of flying, which meant no time off for rest.) A cold front had just entered the area, and Reid had already received a weather briefing advising him of moderate icing conditions, turbulence, and IFR (instrument flight rules) precautions. Seemingly unperturbed by the conditions, Lloyd, Jessica, and Reid proceeded to load the plane to the limit of its 2,500-pound gross takeoff weight. Or so they thought.

Once out on the taxiway, Reid received an update on the weather conditions. Winds were now at 20 knots with gusts to 30 knots. The pilot of a heavier, twin-engine Cessna 414 who had just taken off reported low-level wind shear of 15 knots, plus or minus. (Wind shear is any rapid change in wind direction or velocity. It is considered severe if it is over 15 knots.) Back at the terminal, the pilot of a United Express commuter aircraft scheduled to depart right after the Dubroffs chose not to load his passengers or take off; he cited the severity of the weather.

Whether it was the media pressure, the tight schedule, or just plain lack of experience, the Dubroffs and Joe Reid ignored the conditions, pointed the Cessna down Cheyenne's Runway 30, and began their rollout in a wind-blown rain. A thunderstorm loomed nearby. After takeoff the small plane labored to gain altitude, its climb rate nowhere near the optimal rate for a Cessna 177B of 840 feet per minute.

Then it just fell from the sky. Witnesses saw the aircraft enter a roll and descend rapidly, behavior "consistent with a stall" as the report of the National Transportation Safety Board later noted with detached precision. The plane came down in a residential neighborhood, killing Jessica, Lloyd, and Joe Reid instantly.

The tragedy of Jessica's death seemed to leave the media in a confused state. Patricia Smith of the *Denver Post* praised Jessica for living her dream, while across the country the acerbic Maureen Dowd of the *New York Times* blamed the crash on Lloyd Dubroff's "thirst for celebrity" as well as the failure of the FAA to regulate underage pilots. Writing that FAA officials "sounded disturbingly like NRA and cigarette lobbyists," Dowd chastised the agency for promoting underage flying, quoting one anonymous official as saying that though "there was ridiculous exploitation of her by the media and her family . . . we shouldn't have a reaction to that, so that nobody below the age of fifteen will ever be able to feel the joy of flight." "At [age] seven," Dowd opined caustically, "you should be taking your first trip around the block on your bike. You should not be expected to have the maturity to tell your immature father and miscalculating flight instructor that the weather looks too icky to take off."

Notwithstanding the views of the conflicted media, two hundred people turned out for Jessica's burial in her hometown of Pescadero, California, on Monday, April 15. Her mother spoke, telling the gathered crowd that Jessica knew how "to reach into your soul and stay there." Jessica's nine-year-old brother had planned to fly over the service, but was grounded by bad weather. A funeral mass had been held for Joe Reid the previous day, attracting five hundred people to a vigil for him that evening. Lloyd Dubroff's services were held on April 16.

The reactions of the NTSB and FAA were far more dispassionate. The NTSB report not only concluded that the Cessna was eighty-four pounds over the maximum limit at takeoff, but that the "density altitude was higher than he (Reid) was accustomed to." The actual altitude of Cheyenne's airport is around 5,000 feet; density altitude refers to weather conditions that produce air density similar to higher elevations, thus affecting lift. Cheyenne's density altitude that day was 6,670 feet. Reid, accustomed to flying at sea level in California, may not have had enough knowledge of density altitude to adjust the gross takeoff weight of the aircraft. The NTSB report concluded:

> The pilot-in-command's improper decision to take off in deteriorating weather conditions when the airplane was overweight and when the density altitude was higher than he was accustomed to, resulted in a stall caused by failure to maintain airspeed. Contributing to the pilot-in-command's decision to take off was a desire to adhere to an overly ambitious itinerary, in part, because of media commitments.

On April 12 the Federal Aviation Administration announced it was going to review its rules allowing anyone, regardless of age, to take control of a plane if a licensed pilot is present. On July 23, 1996, the House of Representatives passed legislation forbidding a licensed pilot from turning over an airplane's controls to a child trying to set an aviation record.

In the meantime, Jessica's mother and stepmother had been squabbling about the payout on Lloyd's life insurance policies, notwithstanding the fact that Lloyd had named them equal beneficiaries. A judge in Redwood City, California, ultimately affirmed this on December 20, 1997, after Melinda Dubroff had sought a greater share, claiming community property laws. Lisa Hathaway had counter-sued for child support.

The final word on the entire Jessica Dubroff tragedy, however, might have been spoken months earlier, and in a way almost unwitting in the casualness with which it was delivered. At Jessica's funeral on April 15, Lisa Hathaway mentioned that the attempt at the record had already failed on the flight's first leg from Half Moon Bay. "Reid had taken over several times," according to Hathaway. The haste with which they had departed Cheyenne was not necessary after all.

The Bermuda Triangle of the Rockies?

Although the area in and around Aspen, Colorado, is better known as a playground for the rich, famous, and wannabes in either category, pilots tend to view it as something else: a potentially dangerous place to fly into and out of, even in favorable conditions. Over the past forty-one years there have been more than 322 plane crashes within fifty miles of the trendy mountain town, killing scores of passengers and pilots. Although it is beyond the scope of this book to rank localities in the American West according to number of air accidents, the Aspen area is often singled out for its challenges to both professional and amateur pilots.

One of the most bizarre and unexplained crashes occurred on April 2, 1997, when an Air Force A-10 Thunderbolt pilot out of Arizona abruptly left his formation, broke off radio contact, and disappeared somewhere over Colorado. It was only when the snows receded later that summer that the wreckage of the plane was found on Gold Dust Peak near Aspen. Mysteriously, the attack aircraft's payload of two five-hundred-pound bombs was never recovered— and remain missing to this day. The uncertain conclusion of the Air Force investigation was that the pilot, Captain Craig Button, had committed "spontaneous" or "unpremeditated" suicide, although there was absolutely no evidence of his inclination to do so—no letters to his family, no indication to his colleagues that he was unusually despondent or disturbed. Furthermore, investigators concluded there were no mechanical problems with the plane or evidence that Button was trying to steal the plane in some James Bond–like type of caper. Not only was there no evidence of drugs or alcohol in Button's recovered body, he was apparently in full control of the aircraft until the moment of impact. The explanation for the crash thus remains in the hands of the inconclusive report of the Air Force investigation team and conspiracy theorists who believe he was passing the bombs to embedded terrorists.

Aspen-Pitkin County Airport sits alongside Route 82, the one and only year-round road in and out of Aspen, and that tells you something right off the bat. Situated in a tight, narrow valley, the airport consists of one runway, 7,006 feet long by 100 feet wide, oriented along the Roaring Fork Valley, northwest to southeast. If you're cross-country skiing from nearby Snowmass to Aspen on a clear winter day, the sound of jet aircraft landing and taking off starts to build in a gentle way, not unlike the sound you hear when approaching an unexpected waterfall in a wilderness. But it's not until you cross the final, steep ridge that at last you see the airport, below you as you look toward Aspen in the distance. Tucked behind the steep ridgeline is the airport, tidy with its flight line of Gulfstreams, Citations, Beechcrafts, and Hawkers, sitting idle on the tarmac like so many sleeping swallows.

No aircraft with a wingspan of ninety-six feet or more is permitted to land at Aspen, making the aircraft of choice for two of the three airlines that serve the airport the BAE-146, a stubby, four-engine, high-wing jet that looks more suited to hauling cargo than passengers. Still, its configuration might be ideal for Aspen; it is designed for short takeoffs and landings, and its four engines provide the power needed "to get out of the hole Aspen is in," according to a veteran commercial pilot. Commercial pilots are also required to undergo special training to fly into and out of Aspen, which may explain why there have been so few airline accidents there over the years. (The only recent commercial accident of note involved a United Express BAE-146 that slid off the runway in 1998, injuring no one.) Significantly, no such training is required for private pilots, or even pilots of charter aircraft that approach the BAE-146 in size, weight, and capacity.

As if weather and terrain were not concern enough, aircraft on approach are required to descend quickly from an altitude of no less than 2,500 feet above the Roaring Fork Valley to comply with noise abatement guidelines. Also to minimize noise, aircraft on departure are to make a thirty-degree turn to the right following takeoff and hold the heading for at least two miles. The airport is subject to a curfew, closing to most aircraft thirty minutes after sunset. (The tower is closed from 11 p.m. to 7 a.m.) Indeed, aeronautical charts specifically recommend that inexperienced pilots not attempt to land after dark.

An aircraft professional familiar with Aspen could not possibly imagine a more nightmarish scenario than an inexperienced charter pilot attempting to beat the curfew in a snowstorm, but that's exactly what happened on the evening of March 29, 2001, resulting in Aspen's worst air disaster ever.

Aircraft #N303GA was a Gulfstream III, a twin-engine corporate jet nearly as big as a BAE-146. It was owned by Airbourne Charter, Inc., and operated by Avjet Corporation of Burbank, California, a reputable charter company. Sometime around noon, Pacific time on March 29, pilot Robert Frisbee and copilot Peter Kowalczyk arrived at the Avjet facility at the Burbank-Glendale-Pasadena airport, where witnesses reported that they checked weather forecasts for Aspen and inspected the Gulfstream. A little while later Kowalczyk contacted the Hawthorne, California, Automated Flight Service Station where a weather specialist briefed him on National Weather Service forecasts for the route as well as for Aspen in particular. The specialist also advised the first officer that the approach procedure had been updated and that circling minimums were no longer authorized at night. In the meantime, Frisbee had filed the flight plan, listing Garfield County Regional airport in Rifle, Colorado, as the alternate airport should weather or curfew prevent them from landing in Aspen.

At about 2:30 p.m. Frisbee and Kowalczyk, now joined by flight attendant Catherine Naranjo, departed Burbank for Los Angeles International Airport (LAX), where they were to pick up the charter's fifteen passengers. Upon arrival at LAX, however, the crew discovered that the passengers hadn't yet arrived, prompting them to consult with several other Avjet employees about the schedule, since it was already past 4:00 p.m. in Colorado and the flight—once the passengers had shown up and boarded—would take a little longer than an hour and a half. Eventually the passengers, who were friends and employees of film producer Robert Vajna (not aboard the flight), arrived, and the Gulfstream reported "wheels up" at 4:11 p.m. Pacific, 5:11 p.m. mountain time.

The U.S. Naval Observatory reported the official time of sunset in Colorado that day as 6:28 p.m. Based on a flight time of one hour and thirty-five minutes, the Gulfstream would beat the curfew by only twelve minutes if all went according to plan. It would be close. Having to fly into the alternate airport at Rifle would mean a nearly two-hour drive to Aspen in the snow. It would mean canceled dinner reservations. It would mean an angry client.

Conversation later picked up on the cockpit voice recorder clearly demonstrated the crew's concern over making it to Aspen on time. If the recommendations of Aspen airport officials were being followed, the path of least resistance for aircraft approaching from the west would be to fly over Glenwood Springs, Carbondale, and Basalt—in other words, right down Route 82. Somewhere along the way, Frisbee remarked, "Well, there's the edge of night right there." The time was 6:31 p.m. He mentioned he would have to land by "about seven o'clock." At 6:37, Kowalcyzk queried Frisbee about landing details. The pilot replied that they would have only one chance to land in Aspen. "We're not going to have a bunch of extra gas so we only get to shoot it [land] once and then [failing that] we're going to Rifle." The copilot then read back the wind, visibility, sky condition, and temperature information at Aspen, which Frisbee acknowledged.

At 6:44, Kowalcyzk made his first contact with Aspen approach control. Over that frequency he picked up the request of another aircraft, a Canadair Challenger, for another approach to the airport, which was granted. Frisbee asked the controller at Aspen whether the Challenger pilot was practicing takeoffs and landings, or had missed the runway in his first pass at a landing in the diminishing light of the airfield. The controller replied that the Challenger had indeed aborted a landing, and furthermore, that two other aircraft were on approach to Aspen ahead of Frisbee's Gulfstream. Frisbee and Kowalcyzk were then given coordinates to begin their approach sequence to the airport.

At this point, communication between the Gulfstream's pilot and copilot started to show signs of breaking down, wishful thinking about successfully making the airport before curfew overcoming common sense. At 6:45, they were having difficulty figuring out exactly where they were, trying to locate and follow Highway 82 below. At 6:47, Frisbee admitted he didn't "know the terrain well enough" for a visual landing. Kowalcyzk then remarked that a Lear jet pilot they had met in Aspen on one of their previous trips stated "he could see the airport and not see it." This was met by silence from Frisbee.

Finally, at about 6:49, the Gulfstream pilots had the highway in sight, if briefly. They prepared for their approach. Then the highway disappeared behind clouds. Six seconds later, Frisbee indicated they would proceed on the same path toward the airport regardless, saying that "oh I mean we'll shoot it from here but we only get to do it once." In an effort to quell the possible disappointment of the passengers, he then advised flight attendant Catherine Naranjo they would proceed to Rifle only if they had to abort the landing at Aspen. When the controller at Aspen informed the crew of yet another missed approach to the airport, this time by yet a different Canadair Challenger, Frisbee said, "That's not good." Still, he proceeded on toward Runway 33.

If all this was not distraction enough, at about 6:55 Naranjo asked whether a male passenger could sit in the jumpseat in the cockpit for the landing. Evidently this request was granted, because a short time later the cockpit voice recorder picked up a sound, according to the NTSB report, "consistent with a seat belt buckle."

Two minutes later, the flight crew was instructed to switch over from the approach controller to the "local controller," who was in charge of the final landing approach to Aspen. The local controller informed Frisbee and Kowalcyzk they were following the first Canadair Challenger to have missed the runway ten minutes earlier. At 6:58 the controller asked the pilot of the Challenger if he had the airport in sight. "Negative. Going around," was the reply. Again. An unidentified voice in the cockpit—perhaps the passenger in the jumpseat—was heard to ask, "Are we clear?" Frisbee replied, saying, "Not yet. The guy in front of us didn't make it either."

Still, the crew of the Gulfstream continued with the landing protocol as if all was well. At 6:59 Frisbee called for Kowalcyzk to lower the landing gear, which was later affirmed on the cockpit flight recorder with two "clunks." A "click" and a clunk a few seconds later indicated that the flaps had been lowered. An unidentified male voice in the cockpit said simply, "Snow." Frisbee then said, "I'm breaking out," suggesting that the Gulfstream was out of the clouds and had regained sight of the airport. He asked the local controller if the runway lights were all the way up. "Affirmative," the controller replied. "They're on high."

At about 7:00—just past the curfew—Frisbee asked his first officer whether he could see the runway. According to the NTSB report, this was met with an unintelligible response from Kowalcyzk. Three seconds later, Frisbee asked Kowalcyzk if he could see Highway 82,

NOT TO BE USED FOR NAVIGATION.

Aerial of Aspen/Pitkin County airport, looking southeast toward the town of Aspen, from the official report of the National Transportation Safety Board. Paralleling the runway and taxiways on the right is four-lane Highway 82, which on a snowy evening can confuse pilots. (National Transportation Safety Board) to which the first officer replied in the affirmative. The local controller then asked the crew whether they had the runway in sight. Two seconds later, the crew responded simultaneously, "Affirmative" and "Yes, now yeah we do." Kowalcyczk said the airport was to the right of the Gulfstream. Radar data, though, indicated the airport was in fact to the left of the airplane.

Assuming they were proceeding on a normal approach, the crew unwittingly listened to automatic callouts every time the Gulfstream descended one hundred feet, believing they were on course for Runway 33. But they were not. As if the crew had suddenly realized their error, the cockpit voice recorder picked up the sound of accelerating engines and a steep bank to the left at about 7:02. As the NTSB report concluded,

> The airplane crashed into terrain while in a steep left bank about 2,400 feet short of the runway 15 threshold, 300 feet to the right (west) of the runway centerline and 100 feet above the runway threshold elevation. The accident occurred at 39 degrees 14.315 minutes north latitude and 106 degrees 52.637 minutes west longitude. The time of the accident was 34 minutes after the official sunset.

The crash occurred near the shoulder of busy Highway 82, scattering debris and body parts over the road and horrifying drivers. One witness to the crash, Tim Jackson of Denver, told the *Denver Post* he saw the plane burst into flames and crash, ejecting two passengers—still in their seats—onto the side of the highway. "It looked like they just fell out of the sky and landed on the shoulder there," recalled Jackson, one of the first people at the scene. Another witness to the aftermath of the crash was Colorado governor Bill Owens, who flew over the scene on his way to a meeting of Republican governors in Aspen. "How easily that could have befallen any of us," he remarked upon landing. "It reminds you of how dangerous air travel can be in high mountain airports."

Firefighters and paramedics soon arrived at the scene, shut down Highway 82, and began an ultimately fruitless search for survivors. "It was pretty gruesome, a lot of ripped apart bodies spread throughout the side of the hill," recalled one firefighter. "Thank God . . . it was quick. They died without even having a chance to yell."

Although crews worked throughout the night to recover the bodies, by morning the crash site was still littered with debris from the disintegrated Gulfstream. Highway 82 had reopened, but traffic was still reduced to a single lane. The grim work was traumatic to the response team, many of whom declined to speak with the media. "There are a lot of people impacted by going out to this scene," said a two-year veteran of fire rescue at the airport. "You really can't be prepared for something like this. We've had deaths and tragedies, but never this big." Pennsylvania governor Tom Ridge, who had arrived in Aspen the preceding day, tried to put the crash in perspective. "We're mindful that while we believe politics and public policy are important, we remember that there are eighteen families out there grieving."

The National Transportation Safety Board report ultimately cited pilot error as the principal cause of the crash, for although both Frisbee and Kowalcyzk had a combined 15,500 hours of flying time and had landed in Aspen twice before—presumably in more favorable conditions—the NTSB concluded they had operated "the airplane below the minimum descent altitude without an appropriate visual reference for the runway." In other words, the crew was guessing as to the location of the runway, and was perhaps confused by both the swirling snow and the lighting along Highway 82. It also appears that the pilots may have ignored a Notice to Airmen the Federal Aviation Administration had issued two days prior to the crash that essentially banned nighttime landings at Aspen in bad weather. Frisbee and Kowalcyzk had allegedly been advised of the ban while awaiting the passengers in Los Angeles. But if the Gulfstream's crew had ignored the notice, so, too, had several other pilots, including the pilot of the plane carrying Governor Owens. Since they were flying into light snow and breaking clouds, it's possible that the conditions weren't perceived as bad enough for the FAA directive to apply.

Speculation—both in the NTSB report and on the part of the press—also suggested that there was "pressure on the captain to land from the charter customer." Cliff Runge, president of Aspen Base Operations, openly questioned whether "the fact that he knew he couldn't go around and do it again," led to the pilot's "decision to continue when he lost visual sight of the runway." Defending the curfew, airport manager Peter Van Pelt denied that the deadline would have affected a pilot's decision making, saying, "I don't know any pilot that would make that judgment call." Unfortunately, for the eighteen victims and their families, it is quite possible that one did.

Firefall: Heroes in the Sky

In early July 1977, Rick and some friends were enjoying the pleasures of Lake Berryessa, a pleasant impoundment east of Los Angeles, when a dry thunderstorm formed near our lakeside campsite. The year 1977 was a drought year in California and across much of the West, and the temperature at the lake was easily above 100°F that day. The thunderstorm didn't produce much except for the occasional bolt of lightning, one of which hit a ridge behind our campsite, starting a small fire. Fueled by hot, dry winds, the fire quickly grew to the point where we realized that our escape route out of the campground would be cut off in the time it took us to pack up and leave. Though we could seek safety out on the lake in our boat, our several cars and camping equipment would still be in the path of the building firestorm.

Then came a sound that is music to the ears of anyone caught in a wildfire: the building rumble of nearly one hundred cylinders slowly pushing an orange-tailed, World War II–era bomber laden with slurry. The bomber circled impossibly low over the lake, ascended over our campsite, then dropped its load with pinpoint accuracy on the fire. With the help of ground crews building a fire line and putting out hot spots, the fire was quickly contained and posed no further threat to our campground.

* * *

The history of aircraft in firefighting since the first crude biplanes has paralleled the development of aviation technology in general, its willing partner in symbiotic, often collusional, enterprises being the military. Fire historian Stephen J. Pyne makes it all too logical in his assessment of firefighting in the first half of the twentieth century; on the heels of the industrial revolution, firefighters increasingly looked to machines to conquer wildfire. Bulldozers and even firefighting trains had been deployed on the front lines. But the most interesting—and romantic—machines were airplanes, perhaps because they could fly out of smoke and fire quickly and point their noses toward a blue patch of sky that meant escape. "Almost from their invention," according to Pyne, "aircraft were seen as a fundamental component of forest protection."

Trying to find some public use for its idle squadrons following World War I, the Army quickly signed on as a willing partner in fighting fires with the U.S. Forest Service. In 1919, the secretary of agriculture suggested to the secretary of war that the peacetime Army's balloons and airplanes could be used on fire patrols. An agreement was reached to experiment with the aircraft on a trial basis, and by summer patrols consisting of an Army pilot and a Forest Service spotter had taken to the skies over California and Oregon. The patrols were such a success that in 1920 the Army and Forest Service formalized their arrangements, expanded the patrols to other states, and upgraded both their airplanes and communications systems. However, the program was terminated in 1922 by a Congress that was not favorable to funding a peacetime Army. Some funding was temporarily restored in 1926, but by 1928 the Army was out of the forest-firefighting business, and the Forest Service turned to the use of commercial aircraft.

By this time, Pyne writes, "The love affair between the airplane and Forest Service had gone beyond infatuation." Airplanes were initially used to drop supplies to firefighters in the backcountry; it was not long before the Forest Service tried "bombing" fires with water and chemical retardants, with limited success. The most romantic use of aircraft leading up to World War II was as a platform for "smoke jumpers," firefighters who would risk their lives by parachuting into fire zones. Immediately following the war, the success of the Army Air Corps in achieving "air superiority" during World

War II became a metaphor for the postwar Forest Service's approach toward using aircraft to combat fires; if a spent fuel tank could be dropped on an enemy tank, why couldn't an airplane drop a bomb full of retardant on a hot spot? This notion evolved into the more successful practice of letting retardant free-fall from an aircraft's belly more in the manner of a crop duster than a tactical bomber, and converged with two other developments in the mid-1950s to beget aerial firefighting as we know it today: the availability of large, surplus World War II–era military aircraft, and the refinement of chemical retardants, informally known as "slurry." Like a small nation declaring to the world the establishment of its own air force, the Forest Service even changed the name of its Division of Fire Control to the more impressive-sounding Division of Aviation and Fire Management.

One of the vintage bombers that had survived into the twenty-first century was a PB4Y2, the alphanumeric designation for a knock-off of the legendary B-24 that had been adapted by the Navy for antisubmarine warfare in the late 1940s. It was owned by Hawkins and Powers of Greybull, Wyoming, a contractee to the Forest Service, and most often piloted by Milt Stollak, a ten-year veteran of aerial firefighting when he was interviewed by *Season of Fire* author Douglas Gantenbein in 2001. "This is the oldest aerial tanker in the industry," Stollak told Gantenbein. "It was built between 1944 and 1946 [actually 1945]. It's a tough airplane to fly. It's very heavy, and there aren't any hydraulic assists on the controls. But it's a good ol' airplane." Gantenbein described the fifty-five-year-old Stollak as a "stocky man who'd pass for a truck driver in his slightly sweaty T-shirt, jeans, baseball cap, days growth of beard." This was in 2001, a year before one of the deadliest summers for firefighting in the West—and a particularly bad one for those combating fire from the air.

Severe drought is a part of the natural order of things in the American West; to which most suburban residents respond with adaptation through water conservation, such as a willingness to forgo a green lawn for a year or so. But in the mountains and foothills, there is no avoiding the direct threat of drought: homes are literally surrounded by tinder-dry fuel; sometimes conditions are so bad that even the topsoil will burn. And increasingly, there are more homes being built in these areas. Contemporary forest firefighting policy is driven by protection of property, the era having long since passed that all fires were viewed as evil. Initiating controlled, "prescribed" burns and allowing natural fires to burn in remote areas are two ways the Forest Service has tried to restore fire to the life cycle of wooded lands. However, as soon as a fire even begins to threaten a community, crews are deployed to the firelines and slurry bombers take to the sky. A drought map produced by the National Oceanic and Atmospheric Administration in July 2002 shows nearly the entire western United States in a drought, including a very large section from the Rockies westward that was categorized as "drought-exceptional"—the most extreme condition measurable.

The 2002 fire season began as soon as the weather warmed. By mid-June a significant fire had broken out along the California–Nevada line south of Lake Tahoe; within two days its smoke plume was visible from space, more than a thousand people had been evacuated from homes and camps in the mountains, and at least one structure had been destroyed. A Hawkins and Powers slurry bomber was dispatched to the scene, this particular aircraft a modified C-130 Hercules built in 1957. As one of the "newer" aircraft in the Hawkins and Powers fleet, there was little reason to question the C-130's airworthiness. But as a contributor to *www.govexec.com*, the government's business news daily, later observed,

> Flying any aircraft at low levels over rugged, mountainous terrain is dangerous. Doing so while struggling with erratic, gusting, smoke-filled winds and strong, fire-fueled updrafts while trying to find a drop point for retardant is even more perilous. When the aircraft is old, lacks sophisticated instruments and is loaded with up to 3,000 gallons of retardant, the risks mount rapidly.

By midafternoon on June 17, the C-130 had already made five drops on what was to become known as the Cannon Fire; at about 2 p.m. it was back at Minden Air Tanker Base in Nevada taking on another load of slurry. Thirty minutes later, the plane was airborne and heading back toward Walker, California, ground zero for the Cannon Fire. Its crew consisted of pilot Stephen Wass, forty-two; copilot Craig Labare, thirty-six, and flight engineer Michael Davis, fifty-nine. After making a trial run over the drop area just north of Walker, the C-130 circled back for its final run, flying perpendicular to a ridgeline, then banking into a steep descent toward its target in a drainage valley. The report of the National Transportation Safety Board dispassionately recalls what happened next:

> [the tanker] flew down the east side of the drainage val-
> ley and proceeded to make a 1/2 salvo fire retardant drop.
> Just prior to completion of the drop, the nose of the air-
> plane appeared to rise and the airplane started to initially
> arrest its descent and to level out. The nose of the plane
> then continued to rise towards a nose-up attitude and al-
> most at the completion of the 1/2 salvo fire retardant drop,
> the airplane's wings folded upwards and detached from the
> fuselage at the center wing . . . location. After the wings
> separated, the fuselage continued to travel in the direc-
> tion of the intended flight path . . .

"We heard a 'mayday' call and then nothing," reported Nevada Division of Forestry chief Steve Robinson. Any hope that the crew may have survived the crash was quickly dismissed by eyewitnesses on the ground. "[It] came down almost like a torpedo," recalled local lodge owner Mary Fesko. "It lost both its wings on the way down and it was on fire. . . . We're praying for whoever was on the plane." The crash occurred within 150 feet of Mike's Auto and Truck on U.S. Highway 395, nearly sending the tail section of the plane into the shop. Eyewitness accounts of the crash, however, were not necessary for those not on the scene to form a picture of the calamity; a camera crew from KOLO-TV in Reno had captured nearly the entire event on video, which made its way to the major network news broadcasts that evening. The horrifying sight of the C-130's wings collapsing, followed by the plane's fuselage knifing into the forest, was played over and over again as though we were observing some once-in-a-lifetime freak accident. Unfortunately, we were not.

Following a tanker crash anywhere in the country, Hawkins and Powers pilot Milt Stollak would call either his daughter, wife, or ex-wife, to let them know that it was "not me," to which he might brusquely add: "Got to go. Talk later." A former Hollywood stunt pilot, Stollak passed up an opportunity to pilot for his musical hero, Jimmy Buffett, because it would interfere with flying tankers. Friends recalled that he loved life, women, and airplanes, not necessarily in that order. "When I first met him I didn't like his attitude and his language," his wife Tina Craddock said. "But I went out with him and loved him." The skipper of the Hawkins and Powers PB4Y2, however, may have seen enough as fires intensified throughout the West in the summer of 2002. "As soon as I get my replacement, I'm coming home," he told his daughter Brandi.

Colorado was hit unusually hard by fires that summer, the most notorious being the Hayman Fire in the central part of the state, whose cause was the most insidious type of arson: a Forest Service employee's revenge against a former lover. But the deadliest fire in the state that year was a relatively small blaze started innocently enough by a Jeep's malfunctioning catalytic converter just off the access road to a small community south of Estes Park known as Big Elk Meadows. Although the fire covered only four thousand acres—moderate by Western standards—up to seven hundred homes were immediately threatened. Hawkins and Powers dispatched its PB4Y2 to nearby Jefferson County Airport (informally known as "Jeffco") outside Denver to handle the slurry drops, along with two other tankers and a helicopter. Befitting a calamity occurring on the fringes of a significant metropolitan area, members of the media could not only be found in abundance in and around Big Elk Meadows, but also at Jeffco to record the seemingly round-the-clock takeoffs and landings of the tankers. "This is a very tasking job," one fellow pilot said of the aerial crews. "They're up at nine a.m. and don't stop until a half-hour after sunset. With the high altitude, high temperatures, and heavy load, it's like driving your automobile on a sheet of ice all day long . . . you can get worn out at the end of the day."

Deferring to fellow pilot Rick Schwartz, thirty-nine, of Ulm, Montana, Stollak took the copilot's seat on July 23 for numerous runs at the rapidly growing fire, whose smoke plume at one point reached 22,000 feet. At about 6:15 p.m., they guided the PB4Y2 down Jeffco's runway for the last drop of the day. Observers on the ground noticed nothing unusual about the aircraft, which proceeded directly northwestward toward the fire some thirty miles away. On the scene, the pilot of a Forest Service lead plane (one which directs tankers to their drops) observed that "conditions were perfect for a tanker drop . . . no turbulence and no smoke in that area" as he guided the two other tankers and the helicopter on their tanker runs. Stollak and Schwartz's PB4Y2 was circling the blaze and awaiting instructions from the Forest Service lead by about 6:35. After making contact, the Forest Service plane came alongside the PB4Y2 to guide it to its drop, a forested hillside several hundred yards from busy U.S. 36. The Forest Service pilot informed Schwartz and Stollak that the drop would require a steep "pitch over" just before the attack run. The mountainous terrain in the area varies anywhere from 7,500 to 8,500 feet; radar data indicates the PB4Y2's

Patrick Karnahan's tribute to pilots Stollak and Schwartz, a painting titled "Requiem for a Heavy: The Last Flight of 123." (Reprinted with permission of the artist)

last altitude as 8,500 feet, putting it virtually "on the deck" and requiring the kind of tight, nimble turns that can stress a fifty-year-old aircraft.

The Forest Service pilot's instructions to the PB4Y2's pilots was the last contact anyone had with the aircraft (cockpit voice recorders were not in use at the time). After the plane made its prescribed, steep bank, the pilot of a departing tanker reported that the left wing had come off the PB4Y2. Witnesses on the ground described the wing as "folding upward" and severing at the "left-wing fuselage point." In a frightening reprisal of the C-130 crash a month earlier in California, the fuselage then corkscrewed into the nearby woods and exploded into a fireball. A witness on the ground approximately six miles away caught the entire sequence on a digital camera. Another witness, Scott Fisher, said, "When it came out [of its turn] it was really low and I was like 'Here he comes, he's gonna come in.' And at about that time, the wings folded off of it, the fuselage busted in half, and exploded in midair. And there's a guy standing right next to me and we were both watching and just . . . oh my God."

The crash started numerous spot fires near U.S. 36, which was immediately closed to traffic. Not only were personnel anxious to determine whether Stollak and Schwartz had survived, but there was real concern about another major blaze developing in the 93°F heat. Fortunately for property owners, the hot spots were quickly extinguished; unfortunately for the pilots' survivors, the scene of devastation made it impossible for anyone to believe that Schwartz and Stollak could still be alive.

Back in California, Milt Stollak's daughter Brandi knew he was dead before anyone had to tell her; the reassuring phone call—"Not me, gotta go"—had not come this time. After calling the tanker base and confirming her worst fears, she went to the garage and sat in Stollak's cherished 1975 Porsche 914, which they were restoring together. "I loved him so much; he was my life," she told the *Denver Post*. Three days later, Brandi was at the crash site in Colorado, sifting through debris to try to locate some of Milt's belongings. "My Dad died a hero, but I'd rather have him home," she said. Plans were already under way by a number of Stollak's friends to host a small family memorial "with lots of Coronas and Jimmy Buffett playing in the background," but "no religious ceremonies." Per Milt Stollak's specific request, his ashes were to be spread over a nude beach along the California coast.

Cooler temperatures and rain eventually made the Big Elk fire a memory, but the crash of the PB4Y2, followed days later by the fatal crash of the helicopter assigned to the fire, grounded eleven of the firefighting fleet's forty-one aircraft indefinitely. The National Transportation Safety Board ultimately concluded in 2004 that metal fatigue was the culprit in the crashes of both the C-130A and the PB4Y2, also citing "corrosion, age, and poor maintenance" as contributing factors. Stricter safety standards were mandated, and several of the grounded tankers were returned to service. But for Brandi Stollak and the other survivors of the crashes of 2002, it was too little, too late. "It was so unnecessary, and it didn't have to happen," she told the *Denver Post*.

V

TROUBLED WATERS

In simplest terms, the watershed known as the Continental Divide splits the country's watershed in two. As most schoolchildren know, the eastern runoff eventually connects with the vast Mississippi river system, whereas the western portion drains to the Pacific. The snowpack on the divide, as well as on other major western mountain ranges, is a main source of the water supply for much of the region. This is carefully managed through major human engineering projects: dams, reservoirs, tunnels to impound runoff; and wells tapping into naturally occurring underground aquifers. Except for the rainy Pacific Northwest, much of the western climate is semiarid to arid, and freshwater for human use is a precious and closely monitored commodity. Ironically, in the drier portions of the West too much water in the form of heavy rainfall, mudslides, coastal flooding, and inland flash floods can be incredibly destructive.

Still, precipitation patterns can vary from as much as 150 inches annually in the rainforest valleys of Washington's Olympic National Park to 2.5 inches per year in Death Valley, California. The extremes in climatic conditions are further demonstrated by the fact that *Sunset* magazine has identified thirty-three gardening climate zones for the western United States, and many subcategories exist within these broader climate zones depending on altitude, geography, and other local conditions. Available water supply defined the growth of many western cities—Los Angeles and Phoenix would not be the major population centers they are today without massive engineering projects that brought in water from sources thousands of miles away.

Whether natural or man-made, the many freshwater lakes, rivers, and streams that abound in the West are a popular playground for water sports and boating enthusiasts. At many large lakes and reservoirs, visitors can enjoy swimming, fishing, paddling, sailing, boating, and water skiing. Large reservoirs such as Lake Powell host a huge number of houseboats during the summer season where vacationers can live and relax on the water for weeks on end. These large bodies of freshwater, while fun to play in, are quite commonly where the unfortunate visitor can drown or die in a boating accident.

Western rivers can be slow and meandering in some places, feature world-class rapids in others, and abruptly disappear underground or completely dry up during the hot summer months. Paddling, rafting, and tubing on rivers and streams are common ways to catch an adrenaline rush or just cool off on a hot summer day. Highly experienced whitewater runners are well trained and know the hazards of their sport, but some of the most experienced hands have made slight judgments of error that resulted in their untimely demise in quirky rapids. And the geothermal nature of the West can bring another unknown factor into the equation—the danger of hot water from hot springs and geyser activity.

Most state and national parks, seashores, and forests in the West have websites that offer helpful tips to visitors, including how much water to bring per person per day, and commonsense advice on avoiding water-related accidents. The overall conundrum, just like the range of climate extremes in the West, is that you need to take enough with you for survival, but be also vigilant for too much, in the form of heavy rainfall and flash flooding. Navigating waterways in watercraft can be tricky depending on weather conditions, spring runoff, and dam releases. Conditions can vary in the same place from day to day depending on these variables, and it is always advisable to check local conditions daily before embarking on any outdoor adventure in the backcountry or on the water.

Clear, Still—but Still Dangerous: Open Water (Freshwater) Accidents

One of the largest impoundments in the American West is Lake Powell, containing more than 160,000 surface acres of water when full. Extending 180 miles from Glen Canyon Dam in northern Arizona deep into Utah, the lake boasts nearly 2,000 miles of spectacular shoreline and can be up to 570 feet deep when filled to capacity. Under the management of the Glen Canyon National Recreation

The deceptively calm waters of Lake Powell. (National Park Service, Glen Canyon National Recreation Area)

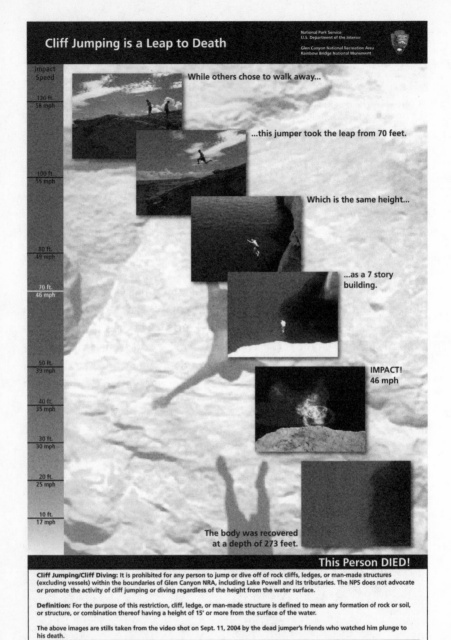

Cliff Jumping is a Leap to Death

National Park Service
U.S. Department of the Interior

Glen Canyon National Recreation Area
Rainbow Bridge National Monument

Impact
Speed

120 ft.
58 mph

100 ft.
55 mph

80 ft.
49 mph

70 ft.
46 mph

50 ft.
39 mph

40 ft.
35 mph

30 ft.
30 mph

20 ft.
25 mph

10 ft.
17 mph

While others chose to walk away...

...this jumper took the leap from 70 feet.

Which is the same height...

...as a 7 story building.

IMPACT!
46 mph

The body was recovered at a depth of 273 feet.

This Person DIED!

Cliff Jumping/Cliff Diving: It is prohibited for any person to jump or dive off of rock cliffs, ledges, or man-made structures (excluding vessels) within the boundaries of Glen Canyon NRA, including Lake Powell and its tributaries. The NPS does not advocate or promote the activity of cliff jumping or diving regardless of the height from the water surface.

Definition: For the purpose of this restriction, cliff, ledge, or man-made structure is defined to mean any formation of rock or soil, or structure, or combination thereof having a height of 15' or more from the surface of the water.

The above images are stills taken from the video shot on Sept. 11, 2004 by the dead jumper's friends who watched him plunge to his death.

Designed for the National Park Service by Glen Canyon Natural History Association

Cliff diving warning poster showing diver jumping to his death. (National Park Service, Glen Canyon National Recreation Area)

Area, Lake Powell is a popular destination in the National Park system, boasting 2 million visitors annually. Not surprisingly, drowning is the number one cause of death in Lake Powell, most often from carelessness or foolhardiness on the part of the victim.

In 2003, for example, the park service reported that the majority of the drownings at the lake were caused by dangerous cliff diving or jumping (also known, in an appropriately macabre way, as "tombstoning"). Although the park service prohibits diving or jumping from any "cliff, ledge, or man-made structure ... or combination thereof" having a height of fifteen feet or more, this has hardly been a deterrent, as its own safety poster clearly illustrates: stills from a video show a man jumping from a seventy-foot cliff only to hit the water at forty-six miles an hour (see chart for relative speed to height). His body, also graphically depicted on the poster, was later found at a depth of 273 feet.

Cliff Diving Speeds

Height in Feet								
120	100	80	70	50	40	30	20	10
58	55	49	46	39	35	30	25	17
Impact Speed (miles per hour)								

Source: National Park Service, Glen Canyon National Recreation Area.

Carbon monoxide poisoning has also been a contributing factor in drownings at Lake Powell. In June 2001, for example, an eighteen-year-old man disappeared while "teak surfing" behind a twenty-foot boat traveling between 10 and 15 miles per hour. For the uninitiated, in "teak surfing" the "surfer" hangs on to the end of the boat (usually made of teak wood), then lets go to body surf the wave created by the boat. In the case of this particular victim, Chad Ethington of Centerville, Utah, passengers had stood at the back of the boat and also weighted the stern down with bladder bags full of water for maximum effect. Investigators concluded that Ethington probably succumbed to carbon monoxide poisoning from his proximity to the boat's engine exhaust, and then drowned. His body was not recovered for more than forty-five hours after some 132 separate dives were made by members of the Glen Canyon and Maricopa County Sheriff's Office dive teams.

Yet another open water hazard is wind. Lake Mead along the Arizona–Nevada border, the largest man-made reservoir in North America with some 247 square miles of surface area at capacity, is particularly susceptible to the strong spring winds common to the desert Southwest. Indeed, an intense wind event on April 15, 2002, not only forced the closure of nearby Las Vegas's McCarran International airport for a time, but also produced waves up to eight feet in height on Lake Mead. Sustained winds were reported to be in excess of 35 miles per hour with gusts to nearly 70 miles per hour. One unofficial recording from the Las Vegas valley claimed a gust of 91 miles per hour. So when park officials received a marine distress call at eleven that morning, their search-and-rescue efforts were handicapped from the start: local highways were experiencing zero-visibility conditions because of blowing dust and sand, and the park aircraft was grounded because of the high winds. The only way to respond to the distress call was to take to the dangerous waters of Lake Mead.

Although one of the patrol vessels was immediately disabled by the rough water, the crew of another in Virgin Basin noticed the bow of a sunken houseboat bobbing up and down on the waves. The rangers rescued three people in the water nearby, only to learn that four more were missing. Two were quickly located and rescued, and the remaining two were eventually found alive on a nearby shore. However, given the rugged terrain, it took a helicopter from the 66th Air Rescue Squadron out of Nellis Air Force Base to retrieve the final two survivors. Because the lake's water temperature was only 58°F, all seven of the victims suffered some degree of hypothermia, and two of those were admitted to a local hospital.

The capricious winds of Lake Mead produced a more deadly outcome two years later, when on June 9, 2004, a mother and daughter ignored warnings about the winds and took to the lake on an inflatable bed. Also accompanying them on the mattress was their dog. According to witnesses, a gust of wind flipped the mattress over, knocking off all three occupants. The wind continued to blow the mattress away from them (it was later found two miles away), but the girl and the dog made it to shore. The mother was never found. Neither the girl nor her mother had been wearing a life jacket.

Perhaps one of the most tragic open-water accidents in recent memory occurred a thousand miles to the east on December 14, 1996, at Lake Meredith, a large reservoir located on the wind-swept high plains of the Texas panhandle. The morning broke deceptively calm for duck hunter Robert Britten, forty-one, and his three sons as they took to the waters in their fourteen-foot aluminum runabout. Shortly before noon, however, a severe cold front "roared out of Oklahoma," and they were quickly beset by 60 mile per hour winds and five-foot waves. Although all appeared in order as the front bore down on them—Britten had called his wife on his cell phone to let her know they were heading for shore—the runabout was no match for the roiling waters. When they hadn't returned by 4:45 that afternoon, Mrs. Britten called the park service to report that "her entire family was missing." Search-and-rescue teams were immediately dispatched and soon some 125 searchers were on the cold, blustery scene.

The body of the oldest boy, Phillip, age eleven, was found that evening. His father's body was recovered the next morning. Still to be found were Patrick, nine, and Ben, eight. Finding Patrick and Ben would prove to be one of the greatest challenges to confront the National Park Service in the history of search and rescue. Charles R. "Butch" Farabee, veteran of over a thousand search-and-rescue missions, recalls, "The search was the longest and most extensive ever carried out at Lake Meredith. . . . The story made national news and dominated the local media." According to Farabee,

> Most of the park staff's grueling search was conducted during blustery cold and stormy conditions typical of the area. On a few days, wind and waves were so bad that it was unsafe to send out boats and the area was scanned from land. Helicopters were used and fixed-wing aircraft flew daily for a month. Diving conditions were so dangerous that only those capable of working in the frigid, dark and, brush-clogged waters took part. Sonar search patterns were run and re-run. Scent dogs were brought in

from as far away as Illinois. The shoreline was constantly swept and the brush-filled coves were scoured after each windstorm.

Finally, three and a half months following the accident, Patrick's body was discovered. Five weeks later, on May 7, 1997, the body of the youngest boy was found. At last able to bring closure to a tragedy that "struck a deep blow to the citizens of the Texas Panhandle," more than six thousand people attended a memorial service, and the city of Amarillo even observed a moment of silence in memory of a father and his three boys.

Though sudden high winds and waves can test the most experienced boaters, those having a somewhat looser interpretation of the ground rules for boating safety can be as dangerous on the water as any naturally occurring weather phenomenon. Indeed, in California alone alcohol is a factor in about 25 percent of all fatal motorboat accidents. Although the blood-alcohol limit is the same for drivers of cars as it is for mariners (.08 percent), consumption of alcoholic beverages is permitted while boating.

In one particularly deadly accident on Lake Havasu along the California–Arizona border during the summer of July 2003, both parties involved may have been drinking. On a Wednesday evening in early July, the Patchett family (Sheila, of Moorpark, California; ex-husband Steven, of Simi Valley; and their three children, Tyler—ten, Kalen—twelve, and Stephan—eighteen) were enjoying a vacation together at a Lake Havasu resort. After spending most of the day together on Steven's thirty-two-foot catamaran, the boys and their father decided to go out for one last sail on the calm lake before calling it a day. Sheila and Kalen opted to wait for them on shore and took a picture of the Patchett men as they shoved off.

Steven was an experienced sailor; Sheila had been sailing with him since he was twenty-one. Several miles down the shoreline from where they had shoved off, the Patchetts' boat was suddenly hit by a powerboat. Witnesses to the collision reported that Steven made the correct evasive move by turning to the right to avoid the oncoming watercraft. Still, every time he corrected his course, the driver of the powerboat, Robert Padilla of Corona, California, veered in the opposite direction, which kept the catamaran in the path of his oncoming boat.

The catamaran was torn apart on impact. Steven was knocked off the boat and killed, although it took rescuers several days to recover his body. Little Tyler was also thrown into the water and, although wearing a life jacket, was instantly killed as a result of massive head injuries. Stephan was not wearing a life jacket, but somehow managed to stay aboard a floating piece of the wrecked boat while unconscious, and survived. He sustained severe injuries to the right side of his face and was taken to a local hospital by rescuers.

When Sheila was reunited with her surviving son at a Las Vegas hospital, he corroborated what the other witnesses had said: that his father had conducted the correct evasive maneuver to avoid the collision, but the powerboat kept coming at them. Police reported finding beer cans on both boats, but Sheila insisted that she was with Steven the entire day and he hadn't had a drink. Robert Padilla, the driver of the powerboat, was subsequently charged with one count of operating a vessel under the influence, and two counts of vehicular homicide.

Stephan Patchett had several surgeries to repair the damage to his right eye and face. Sheila sold much of her family's boating and water paraphernalia, but kept the photograph of Steven and their two boys pushing off from the shoreline for the last sail of the day.

Whitewater Wildernesses:
Paddling Accidents

The adrenaline rush of a rafting or kayaking trip through fast water has as its corollary an immutable scale of rising risk: the bigger the rush, the more dangerous the drop, and vice versa. Nearly sixty people died in whitewater accidents throughout the United States in 2006, about two-thirds of them in the American West, a deadly measure of the popularity sport from Wyoming's Snake River to Colorado's Clear Creek. Paddling accidents happen for many reasons, from fatigue to unexpected stream flow conditions, but those who have analyzed the causes of whitewater accidents have isolated the most simple and instinctive step a person can take in preventing one: go with good people. "All else is secondary," writes Ron Watters, director of the Idaho State University Outdoor Program. "If you have trip leaders and volunteers who have on-the-water training and experience, and who have developed good decision-making skills, then you have the most important basis of a safety program." Watters also finds that good trip leaders spend their free time brushing up on their skills. Furthermore, "Trips are safer by far when all members of the party are watching out for one another."

Of course, even this is no guarantee of a safe passage. Over a two-and-a-half week period in May 1993, for example, twenty-three rafts and kayaks in Canyonlands National Park's Cataract Canyon either flipped or foundered in water flowing at an estimated 65,600 cubic feet per second (cfs). Of these, five were large commercial rafts operated by highly experienced, reputable companies with impressive safety records (which probably explains why the only fatality that May was of an experienced commercial river-runner attempting to "swim" the rapids on his own). Thirty-seven people had to be rescued, and of the fifty-four private permits issued, only thirty-one boats made it through.

American Whitewater, an organization dedicated to the promotion of safe, recreational river-rafting, has over the years developed an American version of the International Scale of River Difficulty to advise potential rafters of the conditions they are likely to face on a given stretch of river, depending on the time of year. Class I rivers, for example, are described as "easy," perhaps still fast water but with riffles and small waves and few obstructions. As one might expect, Class II rapids are a step up, but still relatively safe for a novice with wide channels and medium-size waves. Things start to get interesting in Class III ("intermediate") conditions, which require more skill at boat control such as the ability to paddle away from strong eddies. Scouting ahead is advisable in Class III situations. Class IV separates the amateurs from the pros, with a lot of maneuvering to be done around dangerous hazards. Water conditions may even make rescue difficult should a passenger tumble into the water, so "practiced skills" are strongly recommended. Classes V and VI—"expert" and "extreme," respectively—may best be left to fans of extreme sports or contestants on reality TV shows. As the American Whitewater description of Class VI conditions explains with absolutely no sugarcoating, "The consequences of errors are very severe and rescue may be impossible."

Rivers made full and fast by rapidly melting high country snows bring with them another hazard: debris, which even the most experienced raft operator can't anticipate unless tipped off by a fellow boatman ahead of him. Unfortunately, it was just this failure of communication that led to the deaths of three people on an innocuous-sounding "float trip" on the Snake River in Grand Teton National Park on June 2, 2006.

As stated (or understated) in a national park service brochure, "The Snake is a complex river to float." It continues,

The beauty and lack of whitewater lulls floaters into inattentiveness. A tangle of channels and constant shifting of logjams present difficulties found on few whitewater rivers. Accidents are common. . . . Even boaters frequently floating the Snake should check conditions before every trip, as the river can change overnight. Water depth averages 2 to 3 feet, but exceeds 10 feet in some locations. Boulders and bottom irregularities cause standing waves up to 3 feet high.

Typically, Spring flows will be muddy, extremely cold, and very high, increasing the difficulty of all river sections.

Of the roughly forty miles of floatable river within the park, only five miles (Jackson Lake to Pacific Creek) are considered safe for beginners. Two ten-mile sections, Flagg Ranch to Lizard Creek Campground and Pacific Creek to Deadman's Bar, are considered "Intermediate level" although "swift water and braided channels make route-finding difficult." Fully twenty-seven miles of the Snake in Grand Teton National Park are rated as "Advanced Level": a three-mile stretch from the Yellowstone–Teton boundary to Flagg Ranch; ten miles from Deadman's Bar to Moose Landing; and fourteen miles from Moose Landing to the park's south boundary. Of the Deadman's Bar–Moose Landing stretch, the park service warns in particular that

This is the most challenging stretch in the park and most accidents occur here. The river drops more steeply, with faster water than in other sections south of Pacific Creek. Complex braiding obscures the main channel and strong currents can sweep boaters into side channels blocked by logjams.

Seven miles into guiding a commercial raft trip from Deadman's Bar to Moose Landing on the evening of June 1, 2006, boatman Reed Finlay rounded a bend in the river and suddenly came upon something he hadn't seen on a previous trip that afternoon: a giant cottonwood tree that had evidently been toppled by the swift, ris-

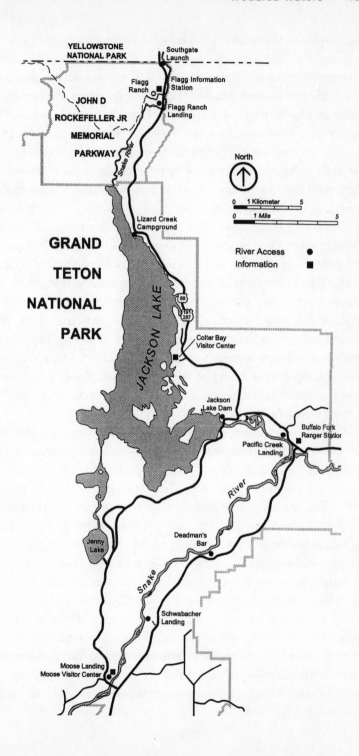

ing waters of the Snake and carried downstream until it caught on a gravel bar, blocking the main channel of the river. The ten-year veteran of the Snake immediately took evasive action and maneuvered his raft around the tree. Upon his return to the headquarters of his employer, Barker-Ewing Float Trips, he posted a note of warning to his colleagues. However, Barker-Ewing is just one of ten companies that operate on the Snake. Unless they had someone out on the river following the collapse and beaching of the cottonwood on the gravel bar, the others wouldn't find out about it until their rafts went out the following morning.

Early on June 2, four rafts operated by the Grand Teton Lodge Company put in to the Snake at Deadman's Bar at intervals of about ten minutes apart. The second raft, twenty feet long and containing twelve passengers, was guided by a college student from Utah named Daniel (last name withheld). Although he had guided trips on the Snake the previous three years, this was his first trip of the season. On board were a group of recent retirees including three brothers and their wives; a former judge from Shreveport, Louisiana, and his wife; a couple from Georgia; and four others. Prior to "putting in," Daniel had helped them don their Class V life jackets and given them a brief safety talk.

Except for a little uneasiness among the passengers when the raft hit bottom in a shallow section of the river, the float was uneventful until about an hour into the trip, when Daniel pointed out a bald eagle nest cresting a pine tree. The passengers looked in awe as an eagle rose from the tree and flew above the raft. As their gaze returned to the river and the raft rounded a bend, however, they looked in horror at what was dead ahead of them: the snagged cottonwood with a night's full of drifting logs and limbs caught in its branches, acting as what professional rafters call a "natural strainer" or "sieve." Seventy-one-year-old James Clark, the judge from Louisiana, turned to his wife Linda and shouted, "We're not going to make it." Daniel desperately pounded the water with his oars to try to stop the raft from drifting into the logjam. But it was too late. The raft was drifting sideways and the raft had to be pointed downriver to slip through the narrow channel to the side of the giant "sieve."

As soon as one side of the raft hit the debris pile, the swift current flipped the other side up onto the roots of the tree. Daniel and his twelve passengers were immediately tossed into the forty-two degree water. Judge Clark recalled that the current "just slammed me down . . . there was nothing to grab on to." His wife Linda was pulled under the logjam and became entangled in branches. Also caught briefly underwater in the debris were John and Betty Ann Rizas from Beaufort, South Carolina. They were eventually pulled away by the powerful current, but did not survive. Sixty-four-year-old Bubba Wilson from Georgia fought off submerged tree limbs as he struggled to pull his wife to the surface. They both managed to drag themselves along the debris pile and safely to shore. After struggling to get to a pile of logs and sticks, James Clark recalls thinking, "River, you're not going to kill me. I have too many people I love and who love me. I will not let you kill me today." Daniel swam over and towed him to shore where he waited helplessly. Linda Clark's body wouldn't be found for over an hour.

Given the remote location, the first help to arrive were the third and fourth Grand Teton Lodge Company rafts. Guides beached their rafts ahead of the monstrous debris pile and started pulling people from the river. A National Park Service raft arrived about forty-five minutes later, followed by a helicopter. Thirty-five rangers searched for bodies downstream of the accident. Still, some witnesses didn't think that the park's response was fast enough. But as park spokesperson Joan Anzelmo later explained, the helicopter was in the process of being inspected and certified when the emergency call came, and the rescue raft had to float down the river to the accident site just like any other raft. "Unless we had our rescue boat on the river at exactly the point of the accident and at exactly the time it happened," she maintained, "we don't think the outcome for those three people who did not survive would have been any different." Responding to complaints that the park should have established better communication among the raft companies to avoid such tragedies, Anzelmo said, "If the raft companies want to set up a system to communicate among themselves, that's fine. But this park is full of wonder around every turn, and comes with an inherent risk. We are not interested in over-regulating. The Snake River can be huge and dangerous, and it can move trees."

Awareness of dangerous conditions has not always been a deterrent for the determined whitewater enthusiast, though, as a tragic weekend on the Illinois River in southern Oregon in 1998 demonstrated. The Illinois, a tributary of the Rogue River, is fed by snowmelt from the Siskyou Mountains, and from March 21 to 23 normal snowmelt was suddenly advanced when approximately three inches of warm spring rain fell on the snowpack. The flow of the Illinois, which is normally between 900 and 3,000 cfs, increased tenfold in a matter of hours, from 1,700 to 17,000 cfs.

The normal put-in for a two-day, thirty-five-mile trip down the Illinois is at Miami Bar in Josephine County; most rafters and kayakers take out at Oak Flat in Curry County after spending some time in Oregon's most wild and rugged country. Early on Saturday, March 22, several groups gathered at Miami Bar, but the persistent rain sent a few of the parties home. The others took to the water notwithstanding the rapidly rising river. Among them were Bob Tooker, thirty-three, and William Byars, both from Washington, who launched at about 10:30 a.m. Also launching that morning was Jeff Alexander, thirty-seven. Alexander was running the river in a small raft along with three companions in kayaks.

Jeff Alexander and his party wisely decided to portage around Green Wall Rapid, and had planned to portage around Little Green Wall Rapid farther downstream but passed the take-out point to do so. He and his partner ended up capsizing in a pourover, sending both into the water. Alexander's partner was carried five miles downstream before she was able to reach dry land. Alexander himself was not so lucky. Although he was wearing a "drysuit," a tightly sealed waterproof garment designed to keep the body warm in frigid waters like those of the Illinois, the neck gasket had been temporarily repaired with duct tape. When Alexander dumped into the river the repair did not hold, his suit filled with cold water, and he became dead weight even though he was wearing a life vest. His companions witnessed him attempting to surface several times until he stopped surfacing at all. They managed to recover his body, and all were rescued by the Coast Guard the following weekend.

Of all the paddlers to run the Illinois that horrendous weekend, only one party made it through to the take-out at Oak Flat. A total of ten people had to be rescued by the Coast Guard downriver from Green Wall Rapid.

The Weather Underground

Rainwater and/or snowmelt that doesn't run off into a stream or rivulet may go straight into the earth and collect in caves and caverns, creating a hazard for spelunkers, especially in the spring. According to Gretchen Baker, a cave safety specialist at Lehman Caves in Great Basin National Park, "When you look at people who die in caves, the most common reason is water." One man's hazard is another man's sport, though, and "cave diving" has become a dangerous but popular activity for the *uber*-adventurer. Still, the National Speleological Society claims that hundreds of cave divers have died over the past fifty years, some of them even fully certified openwater SCUBA instructors.

Although most cave diving happens along continental coastlines, as one might expect, the first dive into a western cave closely followed the very first cave dive in the United States in Florida in late 1951. In March 1953, Jon Lindbergh, son of the famed aviator, dove into Bower Cave in the Sierra Nevada, descending 121 feet. His second dive demonstrated just how dangerous cave diving can be, especially since Lindbergh had no idea how long or deep the cave was, or what other hazards it presented. Though a length of rope was tied around his waist so he could find his way back, two authors of a recent article on Bower Cave have suggested, "The line could also be used for body recovery (politely not discussed at the time)." A small life raft he had brought along had nearly exploded from overinflation, and when he tried to climb into it while in one of the cave's vaults he tore a big hole in his diving suit. He then broke the glass faceplate of his diving mask while trying to bail water out of the raft. After taking almost an entire roll of photographs, he prepared to return to the surface. Though suffering from nitrogen narcosis (a condition common to divers that leads to a feeling of drunkenness) and cold as a result of having torn his suit, he swam maskless back to the cave entrance with the calm and confidence of his father finding Paris in the inky darkness twenty-six years earlier.

Spelunkers can become inadvertent and ill-equipped cave divers when water becomes a brief but dangerous obstacle to cave exploration—tragically so, in an incident that occurred in August 2005 in the mountains outside of Provo, Utah. "Y" Mountain (so-called because of the large block "Y" built on its flanks, insignia for Brigham Young University) contained a cave that presented enough danger to make one wonder why it would be worth the risk to explore a tiny, flooded chamber accessible only by swimming underwater through an oblique tunnel no more than four feet wide. The answer may lie in the ages of the four victims, which ranged from eighteen to twenty-eight. The cave exploration may have been too much of an adventure to pass up, notwithstanding one of the victim's prior experience in the cave and how she had passed out from the extremely cold water. Indeed, at dinner the night before the tragedy the four had jokingly named the cave "The Cave of Death."

At approximately 4:30 a.m. on Thursday, August 18, J. Blake Donner—twenty-four, Jennifer Lynn Galbraith—twenty-one, Scott K. McDonald—twenty-eight, and Ariel Singer—eighteen, entered the cave. A fifth companion, Joseph Ferguson—twenty-six, for unknown reasons decided at the last minute not to join them, and chose to wait outside. Based on the experience of others who had successfully negotiated the cave, the four spelunkers would have walked about a hundred feet through the four-foot-high cave before coming upon the opening to the underwater tunnel, which was no more than two feet in diameter. They then would have had to swim the length of the tunnel, approximately fifteen feet in 50°F water. They would have emerged into a small cavern about six and a half feet in height and able to hold up to eight people in waist-high water.

After waiting about forty-five minutes, Ferguson became concerned that his friends had not yet returned and began calling friends who were familiar with the cave. His alarm growing after over another hour had passed with no sign of his friends, he called 911. A rescue team immediately began to pump water out of the cave, and pump air in. After the water level was lowered two feet, rescuers donned diving gear and entered the cave. Still, almost four hours had passed between Ferguson's 911 call and the time authorities deemed the cave safe for a rescue team. Part of the difficulty was the general unfamiliarity with the cave among the emergency crews on site. They simply didn't know what to expect.

The first body recovered was that of a female, whose body, like all the others found later, was in the tunnel pointed in the direction of the opening to the first chamber. This discovery indicated that the accident probably happened as the four were attempting to return. Authorities further speculated that she may have panicked and inadvertently blocked the tunnel; if she missed the opening to the chamber, she would have found herself at a dead end some six feet away. Given the cold, the dark, and the lack of oxygen, she may have become extremely disoriented and drowned. The bodies of the other three were found in the water behind her, one on the floor of the tunnel and the remaining two floating on top of the water. Although those with experience with the cave said that a rope had been strung from outside the tunnel entrance to a log in the second chamber as an aid to explorers, the swimmers could very well have kicked up sediment, making it difficult to find. And as reported by the *Deseret News*, the four were ill equipped to deal with the cold, raw, conditions: "The hikers were found wearing sandals," it explained, "with the two men in shorts and without shirts."

Following the recovery of the bodies of the four hikers, the City of Provo immediately closed the entrance to the cave.

In Hot Water

The same subterranean flow that can chill to the bone can also yield the salubrious waters of a warm spring as it bubbles to the surface, creating natural "spas" throughout the West and indeed the entire continent. However, in volcanic areas such as the Yellowstone ecosystem, water can become superheated by magma, creating hot springs that are as alluringly beautiful as they are extremely dangerous. The temperature of Yellowstone's hot springs can exceed 190°F—close to the boiling point of water at altitude—which is why the Park Service urges hikers to stay on marked trails, or, in the case of larger features within geyser basins, not to stray from the boardwalk. Adding to the danger is that a thin, brittle, crust of silica or sinter—created from Yellowstone's mineral-rich thermal features—can disguise the presence of very hot water beneath. Benign-looking but equally dangerous "mud pots" can also deceive the inattentive visitor to the park.

Although almost twenty scalding deaths have been recorded in the park since 1870, no such incident has gained more notoriety than that which occurred at Yellowstone's Fountain Paint Pot thermal area in the summer of 1981. One of the most stunning thermal features of the park, Celestine Pool, can be found here, a hot spring whose water varies in shades of blue from cobalt to turquoise and whose depth seems interminable. With all the allure of a tropical coral reef, the pool is a tempting fascination—except that its

Yellowstone's Grand Prismatic Spring from the air; for perspective, the protective boardwalk can be seen curling out of the picture above the spring. Deceptively beautiful, the water temperature in Yellowstone's hot springs can run as high as 200°F. (National Park Service, Yellowstone National Park; photo by Al Mebane)

water temperature has been measured above 200°F. At about 1 p.m. on July 20, two men who were driving through the park, David Kirwan and Ronald Ratliff, decided to stop at the Fountain Paint Pots to have a look around. Accompanying them was Ratliff's dog, Moosie. As the men were exiting the truck, Moosie escaped, headed directly for Celestine Pool, jumped in, and immediately began yelping. Kirwan and Ratliff ran over to the pool to try to rescue the scalded dog, notwithstanding warnings from bystanders to stay away from the blistering waters of the pool. When it looked as though Kirwan was about to dive in after the dog, several people yelled at him in an attempt to stop him, to which he replied, "Like hell I won't!" before going in head first. Kirwin tried but failed to get the dog to the edge of the pool, then disappeared underwater. When he reappeared, Ratliff helped pull him out of the water, and another visitor walked him over to the safety of the boardwalk (Ratliff had burned his feet pulling his friend out). Kirwin was overheard saying, "That was stupid. How bad am I? That was a stupid thing I did." Indeed, Kirwin had sustained third-degree burns over 100 percent of his body, was blind, and his skin was peeling off prodigiously. When someone tried to remove one of his shoes, his skin came off with it. He died the next day at a Salt Lake City hospital.

Though Kirwin's impulsive attempt to save Moosie is now famous for its brazen foolhardiness, other accidents in Yellowstone's thermal have been somewhat less deliberate. On August 21, 2000, eight young seasonal employees of Amfac Parks and Resorts spent the day hiking and enjoying the salubrious waters of the Firehole River near the Lower Geyser Basin, warmed to a comfortable temperature by nearby hot springs. As the lazy afternoon slid into darkness, they started to make their way back to their cars, which were parked at Fountain Flat Drive. The moon had not yet risen. At one point they broke up into two groups, Sara Hulphers—twenty, Tyler Montague—eighteen, and Lance Buchi—eighteen, taking a different route than the others. Holding on to each other and caught without flashlights, the three picked their way down an unfamiliar trail in the dark Yellowstone night. What they didn't realize was they were now wandering among the thermal hazards of the Lower Geyser Basin north of Old Faithful.

Coming across what they thought was a small creek, the three held hands and attempted to jump over it. However, they had not only mistaken the creek for 178-degree Cavern Spring, but also had misjudged its width, falling into the scalding waters. Their cries for help were heard by their friends, who immediately ran to their aid. While Montague and Buchi managed to pull themselves from the pool, Sara Hulphers had to be helped out. The three were evacuated to the University of Utah's Intermountain Burn Center in Salt Lake City, where Hulphers died the following day. Montague and Buchi survived, but had suffered third-degree burns over 90 percent of their bodies. Although some, including the doctor who treated the victims in Salt Lake City, speculated the three had deliberately jumped into the spring without realizing how hot it was, park officials concluded it was an accident. No alcohol was involved, and the friends who had assisted them affirmed that the three thought they were jumping over a stream.

The accident also represented one of those rare occasions when the National Park Service is sued for negligence, in this case by Lance Buchi for the failure of the park service to post warning signs near Cavern Spring. The suit was filed against the government on June 12, 2001, nearly a year after the accident, and specifically alleged that "government employees were negligent in failing to warn him and to protect him from the dangers presented by the thermal feature through the use of signs, barriers, or a closure of the area." The case serves as a classic example of our conflicted view of nature; while we want our wild places wild, we also tend to look for someone to blame when nature turns against us. In the case of *Buchi v. The United States of America,* this ambiguity is further complicated by the fact that Yellowstone posts numerous warning signs around many of its most prominent thermal features—just not at Cavern Spring.

The government filed a motion to dismiss the action on October 5, 2001, a motion that was denied by Judge William K. Downes of the United States District Court for the State of Wyoming on August 28, 2002, because the discovery process so far had been "limited." Following the dismissal, however, a "significant amount of discovery and factual development [had] occurred," during which Judge Downes had "personally visited the site of the incident during both daylight and evening hours." Most important, though, on December 3, 2002, the Tenth Circuit Court of Appeals had determined in a similar case involving an accident in Zion National Park that something called the "discretionary function exception . . . barred a claim of failure to adequately protect a national park visitor against a danger presented by a natural hazard." Quite simply, park officials have to consider a variety of interests when deciding whether or not to post warning signs, "such as resource allocation, visitor safety, and scenic preservation," and under the law they are given the discretion to do so. In ultimately dismissing the Buchi suit on February 6, 2004, Downes found that the Zion case "controls the disposition of the present case" and could even be applied "more forcefully to the present case because the natural feature at issue is in a back country location where NPS policies regarding aesthetics and natural preservation are even more important. . . ." Recalling the remarks of Grand Teton National Park spokesperson Joan Anzelmo following the rafting accident that killed three people in June 2006—

"this park is full of wonder around every turn, and comes with an inherent risk. We are not interested in over-regulating"—the courts seem to have given a legal interpretation to her views. In our statutory declaration of wild lands from national parks to designated wilderness areas, the message seems to be that after a certain point—whether it's a picnic shelter or a visitor center—you're on your own.

VI

BIBLICAL RAINS

Ironically, the topographic features that define much of the arid West—dry, treeless canyons, and unfettered arroyos, washes, and coulees—also make it possible for water to be transported at dangerously high speeds and in prodigious volumes. In most such locales, where rainwater can't be absorbed or slowed down by thick vegetation, waters can rise very rapidly, especially in narrow "slot" canyons.

Gone in a Flash

One doesn't necessarily have to be near a storm to become its unwitting victim. On August 12, 1997, eleven hikers were killed in Antelope Canyon near Page, Arizona, by rushing waters from a severe thunderstorm they didn't even see. The well-photographed slot canyon, a labyrinth whose walls are no more than a few feet apart in some places, runs through the Navajo Nation to Lake Powell and has few avenues for escape. Though the hikers—part of a tour group called TrekAmerica—were warned about possible heavy thunderstorms in the area, a TrekAmerica spokesman seemed to explain away the accident by maintaining that "it was a nice lovely day . . . there was no indication this was coming." Witnesses on the canyon rim, however, looked on in horror as a "10- to 11-foot wall of water . . . just came screaming down the canyon. Some of them were standing up above and just had to watch it wash through while others were down below." The incredible power of the flood was no better illustrated than in the "weird, nightmarish, scary, unbelievable" attempt to recover bodies.

> The flood deposited up to 5 feet of silt [on Lake Powell] and left a debris field . . . which formed an almost solid mat of compressed and entwined vegetation likened to wet baled hay. This refuse cover, up to 6 feet thick, floated on several feet of water, which in turn capped a second layer of flot-

The narrow, winding walls of spectacular Antelope Canyon can also serve as a tomb for hikers caught there in a flash flood. (photo by Annie Nelson; reprinted with permission)

sam. The surface of this thin arm of the lake was so thick and solid that full sheets of plywood were placed for searchers, divers, and scent dogs to work from. . . . Rescuers endured large numbers of dead frogs, fish, lizards, rats, and an unexpected amount of both animal and human waste.

Eerily, when rescuers were at last able to create an opening in the debris, corpses would suddenly bob up out of the water "directly in the faces of those looking for them in the dark water." Even the most seasoned veterans of search and rescue described the recovery from the Antelope Canyon disaster as "pure hell."

The atmospheric conditions that had caused the severe storm near Antelope Canyon are part of a seasonal weather phenomenon known as the "monsoon," a midsummer shift in the wind pattern from west or northwest to south or southeast. (The National Weather Service defines "monsoon" as "any wind that reverses direction seasonally." It is most often associated with heavy rains on the Indian subcontinent, which dwarf the kind of rains seen in the American Southwest.) Scooping up moisture from the Gulf of Mexico and Gulf of California and carrying it as far north as southern Wyoming, the air is forced up against the mountains, where daytime heating produces thunderstorms that can be heavy but brief in duration. The arrival of the monsoon is usually welcomed in Arizona and New Mexico, where daytime highs can average in the triple digits, and monsoonal storms can quickly cool down a hot day on Colorado's more elevated plains.

However, meteorological events can conspire to make storms overstay their welcome, occasionally bringing Bangladesh-like conditions to a region unable to contain hours of persistent, heavy rain. The most notorious such storm in recent memory dumped nearly a foot of rain in a few hours on the middle reaches of the Big Thompson River in Colorado on July 31, 1976, sending an 18-foot wall of water down a canyon filled with thousands of campers and tourists. The culprit was unusually weak westerly winds, which are normally able to push storms past the mountains and over Colorado's eastern plains. The winds were no match for this particular storm, whose thunderheads towered to 62,000 feet, and it remained stationary for hours. At approximately 9:40 that evening, the Big Thompson, whose headwaters are in Rocky Mountain National Park, was flowing at 31,200 cfs in places, four times faster than its previous peak flow of 8,000 cfs in 1919. The flood still stands as Colorado's greatest natural disaster, killing 145 people, damaging 418 homes and businesses, and destroying 438 automobiles. Looking back on the disaster, one historian noted, "The Big Thompson disaster demonstrated the necessity of Coloradans to live in harmony with nature and to pay attention to the limits imposed by the environment on life in the Rocky Mountain West."

The Big Thompson catastrophe has been characterized by some as a "millennial" flood; that is, one likely to occur, on average, once every 1,000 years. The terms "10 year," "50 year," "100 year," and "500 year" are also used to describe the probability of a type of flood happening in a given year, but this is not to imply that floods will only occur at precise 10, 50, 100, or 500-year intervals. It is more useful to think of these numbers as odds in a Las Vegas–style wager; for example, every year there is a 1 in 10 (10 percent) chance of a 10-year flood occurring. (Because the odds are so high this would constitute comparatively modest, perhaps even "normal" flooding.) Conversely the 1 in 1,000 odds (.1 percent) of a Big Thompson–like flood occurring would suggest an extremely rare, catastrophic event.

Following the Big Thompson flood, Colorado's Front Range cities initiated precautions to mitigate the damage a 100- or 500-year event could cause, posting warning signs in vulnerable canyons, creating detention ponds and runoff channels, and tightening up floodplain regulations. By 1996 the City of Fort Collins had actually exceeded federal requirements for preparedness, for which it received special recognition by FEMA. But even those precautions weren't enough, as residents of the area would discover on July 28, 1997.

Just as with the massive storm that caused the Big Thompson disaster, conditions over central Colorado in July 1997 included a monsoonal flow of moisture from the south and weak westerly winds. However, one further element was thrown in the mix: the arrival of a cold front on July 27 that added further energy to the already turbulent atmosphere. Since Fort Collins normally receives only about sixteen inches of precipitation a year, a recap of the rainfall pattern that occurred there from about 4 p.m. on July 27 until 11 p.m. on July 28 demonstrates just how anomalous this weather event was. And as it all unfolded, meteorologists and other experts—much better equipped to track storms and issue warnings than their colleagues in 1976—were predicting heavy rains and flooding for the entire Front Range. Unfortunately, they couldn't forecast exactly when or where or how much.

The first storm developed over the foothills northwest of Fort Collins on Sunday, July 27, around 4:00 p.m., moved southward, and was out of the area by 6:30 p.m. Over two inches of rain fell at Horsetooth Reservoir west of the city, but only a quarter inch fell in Fort Collins itself. Ominously, however, the still air "remained humid and fragrant," the temperature remained steady, and dense clouds hovered over the foothills. Following a brief storm that moved up from the south at about 10:00 p.m., delivering about half an inch of rain to the city, southeasterly winds pushed more moisture up against the foothills. Rain began falling again at about 1:00 a.m. Monday, and fell at a rate of about an inch an hour just northwest of Fort Collins at the small town of Laporte. The rain stopped completely at dawn, then resumed at around 8:00 p.m.; again, the heaviest rain fell to the north and west of Fort Collins, often flooding highways and topping irrigation ditches.

Since persistent southeasterly winds continued to push moist air up against the foothills on July 28, creating dew points in the low 60s, weather forecasters were predicting "locally torrential rains" for the afternoon and evening. Some individuals openly expressed concern that conditions were very similar to those that had caused the Big Thompson flood twenty-one years earlier. Heavy storms did indeed begin to develop at around 6:00 p.m., but there was no consistency to the pattern of rainfall: some parts of the city received several inches, but rain was light in southeast Fort Collins. At around 8:30 p.m., however, "extremely heavy rain . . . of a magnitude rarely experienced in northern Colorado" started to fall at a rate of five to six inches per hour over a thirty-square-mile area on the west side of the city. After the torrent let up at around 10:00 p.m., rain gauges in three disparate areas told the story: 14.5 inches had fallen in southwestern Fort Collins; 13.1 inches northwest of Laporte; and over 12 inches just northwest of Fort Collins. As Colorado State University climatologist Nolan Doesken recalled, "This was the heaviest storm ever observed over an urbanized area in Colorado history." And all that water had to go somewhere.

Normally docile Spring Creek, whose watershed west of Fort Collins had been subjected to the heaviest of the rains, was transformed into a raging torrent as it pounded its way through the city. The campus of Colorado State University incurred some $100 million in damages as water swept through its bookstore, computer labs, library, and about twenty-five other buildings. An estimated 1 million books were lost. By far the greatest devastation in the city, however, occurred to two trailer parks located in a low-lying area downstream from a detention basin on Spring Creek. As waters rose to a depth of five feet in just three minutes, 120 mobile homes were lifted from their pads and sent careening down the now inaptly named Spring Creek. Five people were killed as the homes either collided with one another or got jammed under a bridge. Nearby, water topped a Burlington Northern railroad embankment that served as one side of the detention basin, undermined the rails, and sent part of a freight train tumbling into the trailer park. (Fortunately, a tank car carrying highly toxic liquid chlorine somehow managed to stay on the rails.) In all, 141 homes were destroyed and 1,178 damaged in addition to widespread damage to commercial property. Although officials acknowledged the devastation could have been much worse, they also cautioned it could easily happen again. As a page from the City of Fort Collins website warns, "It is a certainty that Spring Creek will flood again—the question is *when*."

Flash Floods in the Lone Star State

The state of Texas is unique in that it lies in between both the Atlantic and Pacific oceans. The result of this somewhat unfortunate geographical juxtaposition is that Texas's seasonal weather patterns draw major storms from both water bodies. The state can also fall victim to sizable storms stemming from the North American landmass. Inevitably, storms coming from both oceans collide and combine over the state, contributing to copious amounts of rainfall in short periods. In 1935, the small town of D'Hanis, Texas, received a record-setting twenty-two inches of rain in just two hours and forty-five minutes.

A report published by the Texas Environmental Center explains: "Beyond the severity of storms colliding, sections of the State lie in areas where storms frequently stall and drop torrential rains," giving rise to central Texas's moniker as "Flash Flood Alley." Watershed soils can quickly become saturated, sending large amounts of water downhill into established drainages or worse, onto low-lying areas. Small creeks can become instant rivers, pushing water across roadways and through houses with very little warning.

Such characteristics mean that Texas is extremely vulnerable to flash floods. The state's flood history is long and involves some of the most costly natural disasters the United States has ever seen. On April 7, 1900, a huge two-day storm caused the Colorado, Brazos, and Guadalupe rivers to flood. The force torrent was of such a magnitude that it burst the recently constructed McDonald Dam on

the Colorado, sending a colossal wall of water toward densely populated areas. The city of Galveston was virtually demolished as waters swept some 6,000 people from the streets. Hundreds were killed.
At the time, the Colorado River was reported to be sixty feet high
and over a mile wide. Fifteen years later, flash floods killed 35 people in Austin and the surrounding areas. "Whole sections of the
city were submerged for hours," reported the *Austin Statesman* at
the time. Houses and entire barnyards' worth of animals were swept
down Shoal and Waller creeks, commingling with human corpses
as they dumped into the Colorado. The newspaper described conditions in Austin as "a pitiable sight . . . not a section of the city . . .
has not felt the finger of death." But these catastrophic events were
child's play compared to the summer of 1922, when the deluge that
came to be known as the "Great Thrall/Taylor Storm" struck Texas.
It remains the biggest rainstorm in the continental United States
during eighteen consecutive hours. The Great Thrall was born over
Mexico as a hurricane, but soon moved north. Six inches of rainfall quickly dumped upon the city of Laredo. Shortly afterward, the
city of Taylor in Central Texas received over twenty-three inches of
rain in just twenty-four hours. The floods that followed caused 224
reported fatalities over seven separate counties.

One of the inherent ironies facing Texas is that, in addition to
devastating floods, it also faces prolonged periods of drought. The
spring of 1957 was one such time—the state had been caught in
the throes of a drought for nearly seven years. So naturally, many
Texans celebrated when the rains came early in April. But their cel-
ebrations soon came to a halt, when on April 17, a massive black
cloud formed over central Texas. Nearly ten inches of rain fell on
the region in just a few minutes. And the rains continued for over
a month, causing flooding throughout Austin and central Texas.
Three years later, an unexpected October cold front brought down-
pours upon the region. The immense walls of water, brought on by
torrential rains of up to nine inches, swept away property valued
at $2.3 million and forced thousands of people to flee their homes.
The death toll ended at eleven. The storm that hit Texas in November 1974 was the result of a similar cold front. Floods swept

through central Texas, killing thirteen people, including a man and his eight-year-old daughter and five-year-old son. The family had attempted to cross West Boudin Creek in their car, which was subsequently swept downstream, drowning all three. The storms kept coming over the next quarter century. On Memorial Day, 1981, a flood caused the drowning deaths of thirteen people and resulted in $36 million in damages. In 1991, flooding in Lake Travis, Shoal, Bull and Williamson creeks led to the submerging of two hundred homes in Travis and Bastrop counties. Acccording to a report published by the Texas Environmental Center, Texas leads the nation in flash flood fatalities, with 612 flood-related fatalities recorded between 1960 and 1995.

This brief glimpse at Texas's costly and long-standing flood history serves only as lead in to the subject at hand, the devastating floods that struck the state in October of 1998 and in July of 2002.

1998

> My eight-year-old son, he broke down crying. He says, "Mama, why did God do this to us? Why did he take everything from us?" And how do you tell an eight-year-old kid—I don't understand?
> —Sandy Eichman, whose mobile home was destroyed in the October 1998 floods, speaking to the PBS NewsHour

Like the rest of the western United States, Texas's story is essentially a story of expansion. Over the past fifty years, the state's population has increased exponentially, with housing developments and brand new cities springing up in previously uninhabited areas. As a result of this growth, more and more residents and property are left vulnerable to flash floods. And although the state may be better equipped to deal with natural disasters than ever before, the sheer number of lives at risk presents a challenge of immense proportions. The floods that struck Texas in October 1998 showed that no matter how prepared you think you are, you haven't prepared enough.

The floods were part of a long Atlantic hurricane season, stretching from June to November. According to the National Weather Service:

> The weather conditions that produced the storm rainfall were dominated by Hurricane Madeline in the Eastern Pacific near the tip of Baja California, and Hurricane Lester in the Eastern Pacific near Acapulco, Mexico. The hurricanes, coupled with an atmospheric trough of low pressure over the western United States, forced a very deep layer of air with high water vapor content across Mexico and into Texas. Meanwhile, an atmospheric ridge of high pressure to the east, extending from the North Atlantic to the Yucatan Peninsula of Mexico, confined the surface and mid-level water-vapor plumes to south-central Texas.

Such atmospheric phenomenon meant one thing. West Texas was in for one hell of a storm. In the early morning hours of Saturday, October 17, dark clusters of thunderclouds heavy with moisture gathered over western Bexar County and soon extended north to Kendall County. There were a few moments of calm. Then the skies opened up. It didn't take long for Texans to realize this was no ordinary storm. Again, the National Weather System provides the technical details.

> "By 6 a.m., the area from western Comal County to eastern Medina County had received 4 to 6 inches of rain. By 8 a.m., 6 to 10 inches had fallen; and by late morning, this area had received about 15 inches. By late morning on October 17, the rains extended into Hays and Travis Counties. The NWS rain gauge at Wimberley (Hays County) indicated that "intense rainfall began by 8 a.m. and recorded 4.5 inches by 11 a.m., 6 inches by 1 p.m., 9 inches by 4 p.m., and 11.25 inches by 8 p.m. At 11:30 p.m., the 12-inch rain collector overflowed.

With such huge amounts of rainfall hitting the area in such a short period, floods were inevitable. The National Weather Forecast Service immediately issued this desperate warning at 8:27 a.m.:

THIS IS A VERY DANGEROUS SITUATION! RUNOFF WILL BE RAP-
IDLY FLOODING LOW LYING AREAS, STREETS, STREAMS, CREEKS
AND RIVERS. MANY ROADWAYS WILL BE CLOSED DUE TO THE
HEAVY RAINFALL AND DRIVING IS NOT RECOMMENDED ACROSS
THESE COUNTIES FOR THE NEXT SEVERAL HOURS.

An hour later, the situation had worsened, as the rains refused
to cease. Another warning was issued:

EXTREMELY DANGEROUS FLOODING IS OCCURRING . . . NU-
MEROUS ROADS, STREETS AND HIGHWAYS ARE CLOSED DUE TO
VERY HIGH WATER OVER ROADWAYS! TRAVEL IS DISCOURAGED,
STAY HOME, DO NOT TRY TO DRIVE UNTIL WEATHER AND
TRAVEL CONDITIONS IMPROVE LATER TODAY! . . . MORE IS
COMING! CONDITIONS IN SAN ANTONIO ARE LIFE-THREATENING!

Meteorologist Larry Peabody told the Associated Press, "Every
creek and river and drainage system and road and highway and the
city of San Antonio are either flooded or about to be flooded."

During the next few days, chaos reigned in these rain-drenched
regions. Widespread flash flooding occurred in the urban areas of
San Antonio and Austin and along the eastern edge of the hill country in the Interstate Highway 35 corridor between the two cities.
The *Herald Wire Service* reported that San Antonio had received
up to twenty inches of rain during the period, an "unprecedented"
amount for the area, according to the city's emergency management
coordinator, Joe Candelario. A four-mile section of a highway leading into San Antonio and straddling the Olmos Dam had to be
closed because the dam was nearing capacity. Ten train cars de-
railed forty miles from Austin after the rains had weakened a tres-
tle. Fortunately, no one was hurt.

Towns bordering the Guadalupe River suffered some of the worst
damage. New Braunfels residents watched in horror as the usually
tranquil river swelled from its average 150 feet to a monstrous three
miles wide. Fourteen hundred people were evacuated from the town.

In the south-central Texas town of Cuero, where the Guadalupe
crested about twenty-five feet above flood stage, the floods were no

less devastating. One resident, Richard Navarro, left his Cuero home at 9:30 a.m. Monday to report for duty with the Texas State Guard. Six hours later, he and his wife (also with the Texas State Guard) were directing traffic about four blocks away, attempting to aid residents in their mass exodus out of the flood-threatened town. The Navarros took a brief break to catch their breath, only to catch sight of something very, very strange.

It couldn't be.

Were their eyes playing tricks on them? But it was true. They recognized the gray shingles and blue trim. The Navarros's home had been torn from its foundation by the floodwaters and was now floating down a waterlogged Cuero street. The couple watched this surreal sight helplessly—and then went back to their assigned task. What else could they do?

In the next hour, three more houses would follow the Navarros's home downstream. More than a thousand people were evacuated from their homes in Cuero, filling the high school and junior high gymnasiums.

The storm brought not only rain and flooding, but tornadoes as well. About 220 miles northeast of San Antonio, in Corsicana, a man was killed when a twister slammed into his mobile home and ripped it to splinters.

"We had no warning," Navarro County sheriff's deputy Kip Thomas told the AP. "All of a sudden, the tones went out and they said [the twister] was on the ground." National Guardsmen flew helicopters over deluged areas, swinging down low to rescue stranded residents clinging to the roofs of their submerged homes. "Those are the real heroes," said Richard Eppright, the manager of a south Texas cattle feed lot, to the *Boston Globe*. "These Black Hawk helicopters went in with rope mesh baskets dangling 100 feet below the helicopter to rescue people."

"Well, I stayed at my house last night," said Victoria resident Larry Crisp, one of the rescued Texans, to the PBS *NewsHour* and the Associated Press. "I was thinking, 'there sure is a lot of water.' The water just kept coming up, and I got up to the top of [the house], and they picked me up."

According to the *Atlanta Journal-Constitution*:

Two National Guard Black Hawk helicopters rescued nine people from their Martindale homes on County Road 245. Although the homes were no longer flooded, the people could not get out because of impassable low-water crossings. "They were running short on food and water, and they were locked in by water," Martindale Fire Chief Billy Colburn said. "But today was our final evacuation day, so now we know we have everybody that wants to be evacuated or needs to be evacuated."

Some flood victims, displaying the legendary Texas toughness, refused to be rescued, even as they were forced to seek refuge from the high waters on their rooftops. "They just waved us off," Pete Durbin, a chief warrant officer aboard one of the choppers, told the Associated Press. "I think I'd be gone."

Human life was not the only life at risk during the 1998 floods. Much of the deluged region is agricultural land. As a result, thousands of animals were set loose as barns, livestock pens and hundreds of miles of fences were washed away by the rain-swollen San Marcos River. Thanks to early warnings issued by the National Weather Service, many herds of cattle had been moved to high ground, but, as the *Los Angeles Times* reported, "The ground just wasn't high enough." According to estimates, as many as ten thousand cattle wandered from their pastures in neighboring Guadalupe and Gonzales counties.

In Victoria, there were other animals to worry about—namely the four-footed residents of the Texas Zoo, which is located in a flood prone part of the city. Staffers had to free many of the 275 animals native to Texas. The rescued animals were housed in four crowded local clinics, more used to accommodating dogs and cats than wild animals.

The rains stopped, and the water fell back to usual levels. But the cost of these few days in October was enormous. Thirty-one people were killed. Thousands of homes and businesses were destroyed. The total cost of the floods was estimated to be well over $750 million.

As they began to rebuild, the victims of the flood couldn't help but breathe a sigh of relief. After suffering such a terrible storm and subsequent flooding, surely Texas would have at least a decade before a comparable natural disaster occurred, right? Wrong.

2002

Will this rain ever stop? The storm that struck Texas in the summer of 2002 had residents of the state asking that very question. When the rains began on June 30, Texans rejoiced, just as they did in 1998; a long-running drought—which had an extremely harmful effect on the state's agricultural industry—had just come to an end. Just the week before, statewide water restrictions had prepared residents for a long, dry summer.

A week later, such concerns seemed ridiculous. Ever a state of extremes, Texas went from too little water to far too much water in a matter of hours. As gallons upon gallons of rain pummeled the state over the next week, the elation that the storm initially brought quickly turned to despair. A headline in the *Los Angeles Times* neatly summarized the awe inspiring amount of rain the storm brought to Texas: IN TEXAS, A YEAR OF L.A. RAIN IN AN HOUR. Longtime residents steeled themselves for the worst. And the worst is exactly what they got.

"I've been here my entire life," said Danny Scheel, emergency operations officer for Comal County, northeast of San Antonio, to CNN.com. "I've been here for the '52, the '72 and the '98 flood, and I've never seen anything that would come close to comparing with what I saw today."

According to the National Oceanic and Atmospheric Administration's report:

> The rain and flooding developed as a low pressure system migrated westward from Florida and combined with a flow of deep tropical moisture from the western Gulf of Mexico and moved over southern Texas June 30th. While not unusual for the region (one of the most flood prone areas in the nation), the problems developed when the system hit a wall of high pressure and stalled over the central and south central portions of the state. For eight days,

the storm system continued to draw moisture from the Gulf—triggering the massive, prolonged rain event.

In the Texas Hill Country, vast stretches of limestone canyons, oak glades, and pastures were washed out. Several towns transformed into watery swamps. Ranches sank from view beneath the surging rivers. The rains continued—and the situation worsened. Over the weekend, the water swelled deeper. The sun occasionally emerged, but it only gave Texans false hope as dark, ominous clouds quickly filled the sky. The rain slackened Wednesday, only to come back fierce Thursday. In some stretches, rain fell at the alarming clip of four inches an hour in the coming days. Usually dry creek beds became dangerous, turbulent torrents. The lower parts of San Antonio were submerged under several feet of water. Observers reported trees, cars, and household appliances being swept away by the floodwaters.

"It's mind-boggling; it's like a nightmare," Comal County emergency management coordinator Carol Edgett told the *Los Angeles Times*. "There's going to be higher water, more water, and it's going to spread."

Authorities, despite being better prepared for a flood of such magnitude than they were in 1998, still expressed despair. "Everything is flooded that can be flooded," Sgt. Allen Bridges of Hays County told the *Times*. "There is no way to get east or west or north or south . . . right now."

Residents who had remained in flood-threatened homes were soon forced to climb atop their roofs, in hopes of being rescued by National Guard helicopters patrolling the deluged area.

The *Los Angeles Times* spoke with Comal County resident Mary Causey, who watched helplessly as her home was overridden with floodwater after she had retreated to higher ground. "I don't have the resilience for this," she said wearily. And this wasn't the first time the fifty-four-year-old Causey had found herself victim to Texas's severe weather. She and her husband lost their retirement home in the flood a few years earlier. "Causey stood and watched because it didn't seem proper, somehow, to leave," wrote the *Times*'s Megan K. Stack. "Not until the river carried the house away once and for all. But as the day dragged on, as the air thickened and water snakes swam languidly about, Causey grew impatient. 'I wish it would just go ahead and float away,' she said. 'Give us some closure so we can just go.'"

The rain just kept coming, somehow. Residents of central and western Texas could be forgiven in thinking they were in for the biblical forty days and forty nights' worth of precipitation. President George W. Bush declared twenty-four counties disaster areas. National Guard troops, helicopters, and rescue boats were dispatched to several counties. Some of these counties reported as much as thirty inches of rain in just three days. Flooding of the Frio and Nueces rivers (and their tributaries) forced the shutdown of a fifteen-mile stretch of Interstate 35 between Cotulla and Dilly. "The county is shut down. We've had cars swept off the road and people stuck in houses," Frio County chief deputy Rodney Lucio told the Associated Press. South of Frio County, LaSalle County also reported high water. "I'm flooded all over the county," Jerry Patterson, the county's sheriff told the AP. "Every crossing I have is flooded."

Authorities nervously kept their eye on the Canyon Lake Dam, about thirty miles northeast of San Antonio, where water levels reached record highs. As the rains continued, water coursed over the dam, creating an overflow spillway for the first time since the dam was constructed in the early 1960s. The water then poured into the Guadalupe River, transforming the usually sedate river into a mighty, destructive force. The spillway—a 300-yard-wide earthen shoot—was emptying into the Guadalupe River at about 55,000 cubic feet per second, a rate that increased to 85,000 cubic feet per second the next day, according to CNN.com.

The Associated Press reported, "The water surged over several portions of the chute and into the trees growing at the top of a canyon before cascading downhill and eventually reuniting with the Guadalupe." Below the spillway waters swelled, increased in turbidity, and accelerated down the narrow canyon toward the towns of New Braunfels and Seguin.

"I'm not going to take any chances," Al Rose of New Braunfels told the *Los Angeles Times* as he and his children loaded a van and two trailers with their belongings. "I'd rather spend a few hundred dollars and get everything out than spend thousands of dollars later."

Canyon Lake manager Jerry Brite said the overflow dumped as much as 50,000 cubic feet of water per second into the river—more than 100 times the normal flow rate. The spillway was designed to be able to discharge water in excess of 500,000 cubic feet per second. At its largest, the Guadalupe swelled from its usual 150 feet to approximately six miles wide. Other rivers, such as the San Antonio and the Colorado, peaked well over flood levels, engulfing several towns in a watery morass.

One such town was the tiny Falls City, with a population of just 591. Though larger towns like San Antonio could lay claim to suffering the most in terms of property damage, Falls City, following the 2002 flood, was—at least proportionately—hit just as hard. On July 9, Mayor Vi Malone signed a document declaring her town, located in Karnes County, about thirty-five miles south of San Antonio, a disaster area. In her four years serving in public office, this was the second time Malone had done so. "This flood is worse than the '98 flooding in many ways," she said to the *Washington Post.* "We have had thirty-three homes damaged this year, compared to twenty-five in '98. We have had four businesses affected and none before."

Falls City is bisected by the San Antonio River, which peaked at thirty-five feet during the week of rains Karnes County experienced. The river is usually between sixty and seventy feet wide. After the rains finally subsided, it was measured at about a mile wide.

Carolyn Bollman, a Falls City resident, told the *Post,* "We began moving our horses out of the barn last Thursday, when the Medina Lake Dam began overflowing. There is three inches of standing water in our home today, but that is nothing compared to the damage that some people on the other side of the river suffered. Some homes had water up to the roofs."

Another longtime resident, Joe Garcia, said simply, "This is the worst thing I've ever seen, including the flooding of 1998."

Fortunately, the residents of Falls City had some degree of advance warning before the floodwaters reached their town. "We haven't had any casualties, because any time there's a big rain in San Antonio to the north, we have a forty-eight-hour warning to get out of town," Malone said.

Other towns were not so lucky. Residents of Brownwood only

had a few hours to prepare before floodwaters from Lake Brownwood coursed through their city. Townspeople frantically piled sandbags around homes and businesses as water rushed through downtown. Lake Brownwood reached over eight feet above its spillway.

Floodwaters washed away a bridge over the river carrying Farm Road 306, a major county thoroughfare thirteen miles south of New Braunfels, and several other bridges were submerged under the usually docile creeks. Officials in Bexar County, which includes San Antonio, urged residents near the Medina River, in the southwest part of the county, to go to higher ground as a precaution. "There's probably about a hundred houses in the area that we're going to ask people to voluntarily evacuate," Deputy Chief Dennis McKnight of the Bexar County Sheriff's Department told CNN.com.

During periods of extreme flooding, sources of drinking water can be mixed with highly toxic substances, such as raw sewage and industrial waste. The flood in 2002 was no exception. Authorities determined the floodwaters had contaminated drinking water in the city of Castroville, so three thousand residents were told to either boil their water or drink bottled water.

When the rains finally subsided, and the sun made a welcome appearance in the Texas skies, the state breathed a collective sigh of relief. But the real work lay ahead—assessing the damage, burying the dead, and rebuilding. The death toll stood at twelve. The property damage was estimated at approximately $1 billion. All in all, not as damaging as the 1998 flood in terms of life and property loss, but such a fact was small comfort to the victims of this epic-length storm and subsequent floods.

Stuck Behind the Wheel—Tragically

In both 1998 and 2002, more than half of the total flood fatalities stemmed from people in cars attempting to make their way across dangerous, flood-ridden areas. In the United States, it's a simple fact: we love our cars. We think they render us impervious to harm, that they hermetically seal us from the outside world. Car commercials show drivers easily forging rapidly running streams, zooming through rugged off-road terrains, and dodging dangers at every turn. There's nothing like a serious flood to prove how false this image of automobiles truly is. In a flood, our beloved cars can be transformed into inescapable death traps.

According to the FEMA website:

> Drivers underestimate how little water makes a car buoyant. Two feet of water will carry away most automobiles, a fact few drivers may know and appreciate. Water weighs 62.4 lbs. per cubic foot and typically flows downstream at 6 to 12 miles an hour. When a vehicle stalls in the water, the water's momentum is transferred to the car. For each foot the water rises, 500 lbs. of lateral force are applied to the car. But the biggest factor is buoyancy. For each foot the water rises up the side of the car, the car displaces 1,500 lbs. of water. In effect, the car weighs 1,500 lbs. less for each foot the water rises.

A report prepared by the Texas Environmental Center asserts that conditions in the state are exacerbated by its many miles of highways and large number of low-water crossings in rural areas. Notwithstanding the presence of caution signage and flood gauges, however, drivers tend to become complacent after a storm has passed and the water level (of say, a foot or so) seems passable. Having successfully driven through such a low-water crossing, a driver may not be able to "make the important distinction between a bridge covered with muddy water that appears to be a foot deep but is actually several feet deep."

A San Antonio family of four tragically succumbed to such a fate during the October 1998 floods.

Richard Hartman of Kirby—forty-seven; his mother, Donna O'Bar—sixty-five; Jennifer Allensworth—twenty; and Allensworth's two-month-old child, Mallory Hartman, were last seen saying their good-byes to friends and family at a wedding reception in Jourdanton, a suburb south of San Antonio. The rains were already heavy at this time, but the family assumed it could make the short drive back to their home in nearby Kirby. When their planned route was blocked by high water, they turned to an alternate road. This was their fatal mistake. The car was quickly swept away in the raging creek.

Accustomed to the sure-footedness of a paved road, drivers often don't realize that once the rubber leaves the road there is no way to control a vehicle, even with four-wheel drive. The family's Lincoln Town Car—a fairly sizable automobile—was carried more than 150 yards from the road, where it finally lay, lodged beneath the muddy, turbulent waters.

"We looked everywhere," Tanya Griffin, the aunt of one of the victims told the Associated Press, after the family's car was found by police divers Thursday morning submerged in ten to twelve feet of water. "We knew something was wrong."

Justin Hartman, of Bryan, the father of the infant and O'Bar's grandson, watched the retrieval efforts grimly as the car was pulled from the creek. When the Town Car was finally out of the water, he fainted, overcome by emotion. Hartman had been traveling in another vehicle Saturday night as they all departed the wedding.

Also in 1998, Kathleen McCoy of Devine was traveling on a Caldwell County road with her two young sons and family friend. McCoy came to a bridge over Brushy Creek that had been overrun with floodwaters. Tragically, she attempted to cross the bridge. Even though she was driving in a large, four-wheel-drive Chevrolet Suburban, the rapidly flowing water swept the car away. It was recovered three days later under twenty-seven feet of water. McCoy and her youngest son survived. Heather Cottle, eleven, the family friend, and McCoy's oldest boy drowned. A grand jury indicted McCoy on a charge of manslaughter, a felony that can lead to a twenty-year prison sentence (March 5, 1999, *Austin American-Statesman*).

"This is a grim reminder that the overwhelming majority of flood-related deaths in Texas each year involve motor vehicles," said Tom Milwee, Governor's Division of Emergency Management, Texas Department of Public Safety state coordinator, to the *Emergency-Disaster Management Journal* following the 1998 floods. "People who attempt to drive through or near flooded roadways often place themselves, their passengers and rescue workers in danger," he said. "As emergency managers and first responders, it is incumbent on us to continually remind people of the dangers of floods and flash floods, especially when they travel."

In 2002, the Sabinal River broke out of its banks in several places west of San Antonio, sending a wall of water as high as fifteen feet through the town of Utopia. More vehicle-related fatalities occurred as a result. The Department of Public Safety reported that a man died Tuesday after being washed off his tractor, apparently while trying to help others in distress. The same day, in neighboring Bandera County, a man died after his vehicle slid into a pool of water and collided with an oncoming tractor trailer.

But overall, the 2002 floods saw far less vehicle-related deaths than 1998. This good news is at least in part due to the simple-but-effective catchphrase the state devised in order to dissuade drivers from attempting to cross flood-ridden roads: "Turn Around, Don't Drown."

And Yet They Rebuild . . .

Once they pick up a hammer and start to rebuild, they
forget about what has happened.
            —Roy Sedwick, Lower Colorado River Authority

We thought, 'What are the odds it would happen again?' Bam!
Then the rains came."

Those are the words of George Kapidian, of New Braunfels,
Texas, speaking to the *Dallas Morning News* following the floods
of 2002. Kapidian had built his house on the banks of the Guadalupe River, knowing full well that the previous home there had
been washed away in October 1998. But he defiantly constructed
a new home in the same spot. Like he said—what are the odds
that the same thing would happen again? The odds are pretty
good, as it turns out.

Of course, anyone with a good knowledge of the area could have
told him that. New Braunfels lies in what is known as the flood
plain—the most likely spot for overflowing rivers to expand to.
With hindsight, it's easy to look down on Kapidian's folly, but he's

really just following a basic human desire to be close to the water. Why build there? You may as well ask a San Franciscan why they reside in a city so close to a deadly fault line. Or ask Floridians why they build and rebuild homes after the seemingly annual hurricanes that strike the state.

Despite the immense and obvious dangers associated with them, flood plains have always lured people to them. We've always put ourselves in harm's way, in order to reap the myriad benefits offered by rivers. The earliest agricultural civilizations in Mesopotamia flourished in the plain of the Tigris and Euphrates rivers, making use of the rich alluvial soils washed down by flooding rivers. Throughout subsequent history, towns, cities, and industries have sprung up on the banks of rivers and waterways. These rivers have given us the means to build civilizations, but they also have the power to bring such civilizations crashing down. In the United States alone, almost four thousand settlements populated with at least 2,500 people are vulnerable to flooding. Dams, diversion channels, levees, and other means of flood control have been devised and built, but we've yet to come up with a foolproof way of protecting ourselves from the great deluge. What's more, running water seems to hold an ineffable aesthetic lure for us. The sight of it, the sound of it, and the simple purity of water is an appealing, inspiring, and relaxing thing for us. Amazon.com even offers a number of CDs consisting entirely of the sound of mountain creeks and rushing rivers.

George Kapidian might have been better off buying one of those CDs. In July 2002, central Texas was pounded with four days straight of hard, relentless rain. The Guadalupe River swelled from its usual average flow of 300 to 500 cubic feet per second to 61,000 cubic feet per second. On Friday afternoon, 6.59 feet of water flowed over the spillway of the Canyon Dam, for the first time in the dam's thirty-seven-year history. By the evening, approximately 84,000 cubic feet per second of water had flowed through New Braunfels, taking with it dozens of homes.

At least one New Braunfels resident had had enough. Erik Lyon, who had moved to New Braunfels since the town's 1998 flood, told the *Chicago Tribune* that he did not expect flooding there again. But as he spoke to reporters from a cot at an overcrowded New Braunfels Red Cross shelter, he was checking ads for homes on higher ground. "Before we were debating it, but now it's almost definite. I think we are going to move for sure," the twenty-six-year-old musician said.

The first floor of the home Kapidian and his wife Mary Ann shared was submerged in water. "The police came knocking on the door at 7 a.m. Thursday, saying we had to get out ASAP," he told the *Dallas Morning News*. "That stretched to the afternoon, so we had enough time to get our important papers and some photos, and move out some of our valuables. But the other stuff . . ." He trailed off. The other stuff was destroyed by the floodwaters.

One would assume that the Kapidians, following this experience, would be eager to move to a safer, less flood-prone area. Not so, he said at the time. "You know, it may sound stupid, but we'll probably tear it all down and rebuild," Kapidian said. "In California, you get used to living with earthquakes, mudslides and other disasters. We can do that just as easy in Texas." An example of admirable tenacity, simple stubbornness, or pure stupidity? You be the judge.

But Kapidian wasn't alone in wanting to remain in New Braunfels. Mike McQueeny had seen waters rise higher than his roof in the 1998 flood. Despite such an experience, he restored and rebuilt his home in the same spot, to the tune of a quarter-million dollars. After the new home was also destroyed in the floods of 2002, he claimed he would rebuild again—with one condition.

"Yeah, we'll rebuild again," McQueeny told the *Christian Science Monitor*. "But this time, we'll be looking to sell. We want to buy property on the hill."

Hilda Hooper, another New Braunfels resident, expressed similar plans to the *Monitor*. "I own the property," she says. "And nobody has told me, 'You can't put another house there.'" Hooper had also lost her home in the 1998 flood.

New Braunfels' mayor, Adam Cork, found the attitude of his townspeople troubling. "The rivers are part of the history of New

Braunfels, so people have a real link to the water around here," he said. "But we have to find a way to enjoy that water without putting lives at risk or spending taxpayer money unwisely." At the time, Cork said that he was considering having the city buy residents out of their flood-prone homes, but such a move has yet to be made.

Earth Movers

"It never rains in southern California." This oft-repeated cliché—like most clichés—holds a grain of truth. The bottom half of the Golden State can often go months without any rainfall. Tourists are rarely disappointed with the "land of sun and surf," at least in terms of its fabled mild weather. But every few years, extended periods of storms pound the coastline, turning the usually sun-drenched region into a soggy, muddy morass.

The years 2004 and 2005 were wet ones for Southern California—among the wettest on record. The rain season in Los Angeles, which ran from July 1 to June 30, ended with 37.25 inches, a figure just shy of breaking the all-time record for rainfall in the city. The wettest season on record was 1883–1884, when 38.18 inches fell in downtown Los Angeles. But the rainfall was actually much greater in other cities in Southern California, especially in hillside communities, easily shattering several records. Pasadena received a whopping 56.06 inches of rain, almost 10 inches more than the previous record of 46.62 in 1982–1983. Burbank had 44.64 inches, compared with the old record of 39.39 in 1977–1978. Canoga Park, with 41.50, barely broke its old record of 40.19 in 1997–1998.

With rainy seasons like this hitting the state, flash floods are a definite danger, just like in Texas. Indeed, California ranks second behind Texas in flash flood fatalities, with 255 deaths between 1960 and 1995. But 2005's real danger lay in the crushing landslides that struck several cities in the region, leaving disaster and devastation in their wake.

What exactly is a landslide? According to the United States Geological Survey (*http://usgs.gov*), the term refers to "a wide range of ground movement, such as rock falls, deep failure of slopes, and shallow debris flows." Although gravity acting on an oversteepened slope is the primary reason for a landslide, there are other contributing factors, such as erosion by rivers, glaciers, or ocean waves that create over-steepened slopes, earthquakes, and volcanic eruptions. The Southern California landslides of 2005 were of course caused by torrential rainfall. The prolonged storms the region faced over the winter saturated the ground, turning usually dry cliff sides and hills into muddy, unstable slurries. The continuing rain served essentially as a lubricant—and when things got slick enough, the mud came tumbling down upon several towns with little warning.

One such city was La Conchita, a tiny coastal hamlet of just 338 people located in Ventura County, a few miles east of Santa Barbara. The entire town is made up of two streets running parallel to the shore and ten running perpendicular. Nestled between the Pacific Ocean and a looming hillside, La Conchita is prized for its private, enclave-like atmosphere. And like any coastal SoCal town worth its salt, the surfing is great.

But residents weren't hitting the waves much at the start of 2005, as rains pounded the area for weeks. More likely, their minds were cast back to ten years earlier, when a massive mudslide dumped 600,000 tons of mud into the town, crushing nine homes between the hillside and the ocean. Luckily, no one was killed or injured in that event. La Conchita's luck was not as good in 2005.

On Monday, January 10, the hillside gave way as a result of the prolonged rains. "It's not much of a surprise that it failed in this spot," said Douglas Morton, a research geologist with the U.S. Geological Survey, to the *San Francisco Chronicle*. "Whenever you have something like the '95 failure, it's very common to have larger secondary landsliding. It's not rocket science."

The coastal hills of La Conchita are specifically vulnerable to landslides because the slopes are very steep and the sand-clay soils they consist of are very unstable. Geologists refer to such areas as a "marine terrace," a region that was once directly on the water but has been lifted up by millennia of seismic activity. The soils in marine terraces, never having been compacted, are inherently loose and sandy. Add to that the intense rainfall from a series of Pacific winter storms, and mudslides are inevitable, geologists say.

La Conchita residents and county officials weren't ignorant of the danger. Signs warning of a potential landslide had been posted throughout La Conchita for years. In hopes of providing early indication of such an event, motion detectors were installed on the slope. Additionally, the county built a $400,000, eighteen-foot-high retaining wall at the base of the hill between the slide zone and the community. But the detectors did not warn of the hillside's collapse in time for residents to evacuate endangered homes. The time it took for movement on the hillside to begin and when the hillside collapsed was only a matter of seconds. And the much-vaunted retaining wall, which residents hoped would keep a good amount of a landslide away from their homes, was simply not strong enough.

"It came down like a big wave," resident Ted Jennings told the *Long Beach Press Telegram*. "It came down like a river. It was so fast there was no time to get out of its way."

Jodi Renz was on the second floor of her La Conchita home when the mudslide pounded into the building, rending it from its foundation. "I looked up and it just snapped," she said to the *Press Telegram*. "You could feel the earth rumble. I heard the pilings crack. The hill just spilled like sugar. It came down so fast I didn't know whether to run down the stairs, or run to the edge of the deck and just hang on."

Kathleen Wood, a longtime La Conchita resident, saw the earth tumble down, snapping the retaining wall. "It hit an old school bus," she told the *Los Angeles Times*. "The force of the mud drove the bus through a home. It was silent and [then] there was this huge roar."

The Associated Press described the scene: "The dirt flowed like a waterfall, engulfing more than a dozen homes in a four-block area of the town seventy miles northwest of Los Angeles. Panicked residents ran as the tons of mud closed in on them; others ran toward the slide, helping some of the injured reach safety."

Fifteen La Conchita homes in close proximity to the hillside were destroyed by this onslaught of thick, brown matter. Sixteen more homes were seriously damaged. Dozens of automobiles were crushed beneath the onslaught. One home belonged to Jimmie Wallet, who, in the hours following the landslide, desperately searched for his wife and three children amid the wreckage and debris. "I know they've got to be there," he said. "I'm not going to stop."

Wallet, a thirty-seven-year-old construction worker, had left his house for only a short while to pick up ice cream from the nearby mini-mart when the mudslide hit. As he came out of the store, he saw the mud flowing rapidly toward his home. He sprinted back, but in just a few seconds the building was overrun with mud and muck. Wallet immediately began digging by hand, desperately searching for his family. Wallet was so driven that at one point on Tuesday morning, he had to be physically restrained by authorities and be briefly handcuffed. "I have to get my kids! I have to get my kids!" he screamed.

But Wallet was too late. Thirty-six hours after the slide hit his home, the body of his wife, Mechelle, was discovered. Firefighters carried her to the makeshift morgue at a local gas station, where a tearful Wallet identified her. And this was only the beginning. A few hours later, Wallet's youngest daughter, two-year-old Paloma, was carried out on a stretcher. Her six-year-old sister, Raven, came next, followed shortly by ten-year-old Hannah. The three girls were found buried in the mud next to each other.

"They never had a chance to get out," said Scott Hall, a battalion chief with Ventura County Fire Department, to CBS News. "It appeared they were sitting on a couch unaware of the slide."

Wallet was the hardest hit La Conchita resident, but he was by no means the only one. Rescue operations continued for several days as firefighters and volunteers dug through the tons of mud, in search of trapped survivors. It's possible for a person to survive up to four days beneath the mud, provided he or she has an air pocket.

"We're going to keep digging until we get through the rubble and see if there's anybody left," said Ventura County Fire Department spokesperson Joe Foy to CBS News.

Rescuers using listening devices designed to pick up faint sounds, such as whimpering and scratching, scoured the devastated houses. There were few signs of life. On Tuesday, no survivors were found— only fatalities. When the cleanup finally culminated weeks later, the death toll totaled ten, an immense loss for a tiny community like La Conchita. The amount of mud dumped on the town? Four hundred thousand tons.

But just as we've seen in flood-ridden regions of Texas, residents aren't fleeing from this potentially dangerous area in droves. Governor Arnold Schwarzenegger told reporters, "One of the first things they said is, you know, 'We'll be back.' I would say that I'm going to help them so they can come back here."

"It's not that we're dumb," said Julio Varele, a longtime resident who planned to move back once the cleanup was finished. "It's just a wonderful place."

VII

The Sky Above, the Earth Below: More Severe Weather, Changing Climate, and the Future of Western Wildlands

On December 7, 2006, the National Oceanic and Atmospheric Administration (NOAA) predicted that, based on a strengthening El Niño event in the Pacific Ocean, winter would bring "increased storminess and wetter-than-average conditions . . . across the southern tier of the U.S. from central and southern California across the Southwest to Texas and across the Gulf Coast to Florida and the Southeast." Accompanying the announcement in *NOAA Magazine* was a map of North America showing the continental weather outlook for December 2006 through February 2007. For Colorado's Front Range, the urban strip east of the Continental Divide running from Fort Collins to Pueblo and including the metropolitan areas of Boulder, Denver, and Colorado Springs, the map was painted a dull brown, indicating above-average temperatures and below-average to average precipitation for the period.

For the following ten days, the weather held true to the NOAA forecast, with temperatures in the Boulder–Denver area even reaching into the low 60s on December 15 and 16. Later that week, however, the temperature plummeted, and a strong low pressure system moved into southeastern Colorado. In Boulder alone, twenty-six inches of snow fell on December 20 and 21, with much higher amounts in the nearby foothills. Blizzard conditions led to the closure of Denver International Airport for nearly two days, canceling over a thousand flights and stranding three thousand passengers. Though major roads and highways were cleared quickly, unplowed side streets stranded residents in their homes and closed businesses and schools. A rare event even for a "normal" December—no more than a foot of snow falls during the month, on average—eastern Coloradans were treated to one of their infrequent white Christmases.

Weeks later, that white Christmas was not looking so special. Just as Coloradans were cleaning up from the December 20–21 blizzard, snow started falling again. Although a little more than 4 inches fell during the week of December 22 (including 2 inches on Christmas Eve), another storm pounded the area on December 29, dumping 12.5 inches on central Boulder. Moreover, this wasn't "fluffy white stuff": the water content of the snow was 0.72 inch, in one storm exceeding Boulder's average precipitation for the entire month. According to records kept by Bill Callahan, Boulder's popular weather watcher, snowfall for the month exceeded 45 inches and had a water content that exceeded 3 inches. For Denver, December 2006 was its third snowiest on record.

Those folks looking for relief in January would have had to go to the unusually balmy New York and New England to escape the snow. The month was the seventh snowiest in Denver's history with snow totals over twice the monthly average of 7½ inches, and the mean monthly temperature was almost 9 degrees below average, making it the seventh coldest January in Denver as well. When the last snow disappeared from the ground in Denver on February 19, it had concluded the second-longest period of consecutive days with snow on the ground in the city's history: sixty-one days, just shy of the record of sixty-three days in 1983–1984. In favored areas such as shaded north-facing yards and higher elevations, the snow lingered until early March.

Eastern Colorado's winter storms of 2006–2007 not only demonstrated how difficult it is to forecast the weather beyond just a few days, but also how crippling storms can be to a region's economy and livelihood. The forty-five-hour closure of Denver International Airport made life miserable for stranded passengers and caused its two largest carriers, United and Frontier, to incur substantial financial losses. Five people may have been killed in the December storms, though uncertainty about preexisting conditions made it difficult to pin the blame directly on the weather. In southeastern Colorado, though, thousands of sheep and cattle died, many while in their feedlots. Businesses were crippled when snow-drifted highways regularly stranded trucks, which even when they got through had to deal with snow and ice-clogged alleyways. Supermarket shelves were empty for days on end, and it was difficult if not impossible to find one valued commodity, windshield-washer fluid, until February. The Colorado experience made fools out of two kinds of people: those who think climate modeling is infallible, and those who think weather and climate are forces of nature that we somehow have control over.

The American West is a land of extremes, which further complicates forecasting. As one meteorologist put it, playing on the old quip "If you don't like the weather, wait a minute; if you still don't like the weather, go a few miles." Just a few driving hours from Death Valley in California, for example, whose elevation is 178 feet below sea level and whose average July temperature is 115°F, is Sequoia and Kings Canyon national parks, containing shady forests and alpine ecosystems where summer ends abruptly in early September. Befitting such proximate disparities in topography and climate, the West showcases some of the planet's most spectacular weather events: scorching heat, thunderheads that rise to over 60,000 feet, winds in excess of 100 miles per hour, snowfall measured in feet rather than inches, devastating tornadoes, torrential rains, and even hurricanes. Without the moderating influence of the Gulf Stream and a topography whose changes are gradual, such as in the eastern United States, it is not impossible for all of these events to happen at the same time from California to Colorado. And although deaths from extreme weather events have been declining steadily since the mid-twentieth century, words written 120 years ago by Theodore Roosevelt at his ranch in the Dakota Badlands could easily have been applied to Colorado's most recent winter woes:

> Sometimes furious gales blow out of the north, driving
> before them the clouds of blinding snow-dust, wrapping
> the mantle of death round every unsheltered being that

faces their unshackled anger. They roar in a thunderous bass as they sweep across the prairie or whirl through the naked canyons, and beneath their rough touch the icy limbs of the pines that cluster in the gorges sing like the chords of an Eolian harp.

Serious Heat

Capping a snow season in which it exceeded its annual average by sixteen inches—ten more inches fell in March, bringing the total to seventy-six inches for the year—Denver recorded its latest freezing temperature on record on June 8, 2007, when a temperature of 31°F was recorded at Denver International airport. Just a few weeks earlier, a storm had dumped up to two feet of snow on the nearby foothills. Within forty-eight hours of Denver's record low, though, the temperature had soared nearly 60°F, reaching a high of 90°F on June 10. Such temperature swings are not all that unusual in the spring and fall in the intermountain West; in his classic memoir of living and working in Arches National Park forty years ago, *Desert Solitaire*, Edward Abbey describes first arriving at the park on the evening of April 1 in a driving snowstorm, only to awaken the following morning to a "flaming globe, blazing on the pinnacles and minarets and balanced rocks." A short while later, "the snowfall has disappeared by this time and all watercourses in the park are dry except for the one spring-fed perennial stream."

For the most part, the West experiences a dry heat, though some environmentalists insist that the development of irrigation canals, reservoirs, and water-thirsty landscaping has increased the overall relative humidity in cities like Denver and Phoenix. However, a review of weather records for Phoenix conducted by the Office of Climatology at Arizona State University found this not true; furthermore, the opposite was occurring—relative humidity had fallen as

A land of contrasts: Death Valley is just seventy miles from cool, lush, Sequoia and King's Canyon National Parks. (National Park Service, Death Valley and Sequoia and King's Canyon National Parks)

the city grew. Explaining this was "caused by (a) paved surfaces that store little moisture and force rapid runoff following a rain event and (b) increased temperature in the 'urban heat island,'" the scientists studied five-year periods from 1895 to 1995. The years 1916 through 1920 recorded the highest average relative humidity at 48 percent; the lowest was recorded for the period 1986 through 1990, when the average relative humidity measured 34 percent. Though temperatures in the Phoenix area have trended higher as former desert lands have been covered by asphalt and concrete, heat indexes (to warm weather what wind chill is to cold weather) have not risen correspondingly, mostly because the temperature seldom rises above 105°F during periods of high relative humidity (30–40%). For example, if the temperature is 105°F and the relative humidity is 32 percent, the heat index will be the same—113—as it is for a temperature of 110°F with a relative humidity of 22 percent.

Although low humidity is not much comfort when the temperature hits triple digits—and it's capable of doing so anywhere in the West outside of high mountain areas—irrigation and air condi-

Beautiful, but home to triple-digit temperatures, Organ Pipe Cactus National Monument on the Arizona–Mexico border has become a graveyard for many people seeking illegal entry into the United States. (National Park Service, Organ Pipe Cactus National Monument)

tioning have made it possible to settle areas nearly as hot as the Sahara. In fact, if one had to identify a class of people who are almost exclusively susceptible to the dangers of extreme heat, it would be illegal immigrants attempting to cross the border from Mexico to the United States from California to Texas. On July 3, 1980, twenty-six Salvadorans paid two "coyotes" (people smugglers) $1,200 each to cross the thirty-mile-long border in Organ Pipe Cactus National Monument. By noon on July 4 their water had run out, and the dehydrated illegals had separated from each other and started wandering aimlessly across the desert. When Border Patrol officials came across a few stragglers and learned that many more were lost among the cactus, "trackers, motorcyclists, horsemen, and helicopters" were engaged to find them all in the 110°F heat. Find them they did—thirteen survivors and thirteen bodies.

A similar tragedy occurred in Cabeza Prieta National Wildlife Refuge in May 2001, when fourteen immigrants crossed the border from Mexico to Arizona illegally, got lost, and died. However, because wildlife refuge officials had denied a request from an organization known as Humane Borders to erect seven water stations on roads within Cabeza Prieta, families for eleven of the victims filed a claim against the Department of the Interior and the U.S. Fish and Wildlife Service, seeking damages of $3.75 million for each of the deceased. Though the case became a cause célèbre among open borders advocates, a spokesman for the U.S. Fish and Wildlife Service explained, "Of those places [Humane Borders] requested to place water stations, none of them would have helped the poor people who perished there. In fact, the closest proposed water area for a water station was 12 miles and two mountain ranges away from where the migrants were found dead." He added that the government had established several unmarked watering holes with 10,000-gallon tanks in an effort to support the endangered Sonoran pronghorn antelope, and that "our idea is to mark where the water holes are as a humane gesture." The United States District Court for the District of Columbia ultimately dismissed the action, once again citing the "discretionary function" of government officials (see "In Hot Water," *Buchi v. The United States of America*). Particularly, the court found, "Defendant's concerns about the safety of aliens (who might be encouraged to cross the area because of the presence of the water drums), the safety of refuge visitors (who have been victimized by a small percentage of illegal crossers), and environmental harm (arising from habitat disruption and littering of debris) gave Defendant the discretion to decline to authorize the erection of water drums on Cabeza Prieta, and therefore the court has no jurisdiction to hear this case."

Of course, another consequence of extreme heat and its periodic corollary, drought, is wildfire. To even declare that this is a common, natural phenomenon in the American West would still understate the tremendous force of nature that fire is. As wildfire expert Stephen J. Pyne tells us in his 1982 book *Fire in America: A Cultural History of Wildland Fire*, "Between 1940 and 1975 a total of 59,518 lightning fires occurred on the national forests of the Southwest, 79,131 on the forests of the Rocky Mountains, and 88,680 on the forests of the Pacific Northwest." Moreover, "The largest episode on record came during a 10-day period in June 1940, when 1,488 lightning fires broke out in the Northern Rockies." (Interestingly, those fires all occurred during a period of global cooling, when moisture levels were slightly higher than normal.) The average annual number of lightning-caused fires—those that are reported, that is—varies throughout the West, from as few as 1 to 5 per million acres on the Great Plains to more than 60 per million acres in parts of Arizona and New Mexico. The intermountain West has the second highest frequency of lightning-caused fires with between 41 and 60 per million acres annually.

Although fire is an important part of forest and grassland ecosystems, only until fairly recently have managers abandoned the notion that complete suppression amounted to prudent stewardship of the public lands. The fire history of the Yellowstone region provides no better example of these evolving views, especially after the infamous fires of 1988 reignited debate over the issue. For most of the twentieth century, fire was viewed negatively in Yellowstone, and it was the park's policy to try to suppress all fires. As scientists grew to recognize the importance of wildland succession, however, by the 1970s Yellowstone and other parks and national forests began to allow some lightning-caused fires to burn. These fires were generally in remote areas away from popular visitor destinations. A total of 235 fires were allowed to burn 33,759 acres in Yellowstone during the fifteen years from 1972 to 1987, and all but 15 of the fires were 100 acres or less. In the case of all the fires, the park service maintained a "hands-off" policy, and the fires either burned themselves out or were extinguished by rain and snow.

By the summer of 1988, however, conditions in the Yellowstone area were ripe for a major conflagration. The period from 1982 to 1987 (and indeed, early 1988) had been wet years, suppressing fire and allowing fuels to build. But by June 1988 the area had fallen into a severe drought and little moisture could be drawn out of passing thunderstorms. (The summer of 1988 would turn out to be the driest in Yellowstone's history.) Although only 8,500 acres had burned by mid-July, the park service made the decision on July 21 to suppress all fires. Within a few days, however, fires were burning on nearly 100,000 acres in the park, a figure that was to grow sevenfold by the end of the summer. In one dramatic example of what a powerful force fire can be, on August 20 alone high winds pushed fire across more than 150,000 acres. With about a third of the park on fire or burned out, some park roads and facilities became inaccessible. Since the fires were impossible to suppress completely, officials made public safety and protection of property their highest priority.

Nature didn't come to the rescue until September 11, when snow began falling in the park, but the last fire wasn't put out until November. Assessing the impact of the fires, the park service reported,

> A total of 248 fires started in greater Yellowstone in 1988; 50 of those were in Yellowstone National Park. Despite widespread misconceptions that all fires were initially allowed to burn, only 31 of the total were; 28 of these began inside the park. In the end, 7 major fires were responsible for more than 95% of the burned acreage. Five of those fires were ignited outside the park, and 3 of them were human-caused fires that firefighters attempted to control from the beginning. More than 25,000 firefighters . . . attacked Yellowstone fires in 1988, at a total cost of $120 million.

Although fires had burned some 1.2 million acres in the Yellowstone ecosystem and 793,000 acres in the park itself, only sixty-seven structures were destroyed. Impact on wildlife was minimal: 345 elk (out of a system-wide population of 40,000 to 50,000) were killed, as well as 36 deer, 12 moose, 6 black bears, and 9 bison. Astoundingly—given the large number of firefighters, support teams, and park visitors, not to mention the outright danger of such a vast wildfire—only two people were killed, one by a falling tree, the other while piloting a plane. Although park officials were often mistakenly accused of allowing the fires to burn in the name of nature and at the expense of safety and protection of property, quite the opposite was true. Indeed, in the years following the fires the burned lands became attractions in themselves, offering new vistas where forests had previously existed and meadows bursting with wildflowers as ash bolstered nutrients in the soil.

As a tragic event in Colorado demonstrated six years after the Yellowstone fires, however, a wildfire doesn't have to be big to be fatal. On July 2, 1994, lightning struck a mountainside outside the town of Glenwood Springs. For the next two days, the modest fire burned downslope, fueled by leaves, twigs, and dry grasses. The fire had grown to 50 acres by July 5 and covered 127 acres by July 6. On the morning of July 6, the Bureau of Land Management dispatched several crews to the fire, among them twenty members of the Prineville Hotshots, a crack firefighting unit out of Oregon. By the afternoon, the Hotshots were working the main fire line on steeply sloped Storm King Mountain. When an approaching cold front started to kick up winds just after 3 p.m., giving the fire new life, the firefighters were ordered to climb to safety. The crew gradually made their way up the mountain, some even stopping to take pictures.

Then the mountain suddenly exploded. Wind gusts of 30 to 45 miles per hour pushed the fire upslope and into Gambel oak; officials later estimated that the fire moved at the rate of six to nine feet per second in the vicinity where the Prineville crew was trying to escape. As the firefighters became alarmed by the rapidly approaching fire behind them, some hit the ground and attempted to deploy their portable fire shelters, foil blankets meant to deflect heat. These, however, proved to be no match for the intense heat, and the shelters simply crumbled. Fourteen firefighters were killed, mercifully by rapid asphyxiation. As writer Sebastian Junger speculated in an article on the incident titled "Blowup: What Went Wrong on Storm King Mountain," "Their suffering was probably intense but short-lived." Indeed, the victims were probably no longer breathing when the fire passed over them. Pathologists found high levels of carbon monoxide in their blood which, Junger explains, "kills very quickly."

Though their bodies were badly charred, most of the burns probably came after the firefighters were dead. Temperatures were estimated to have approached 2,000°F as the fire passed over them

A survivor of the South Canyon fire recalled that the wall of flame reached nearly three hundred feet in height and roared like a "tornado on fire." A follow-up report on the fire concluded, "Three major factors contributed to the blowup. . . . The first was the presence of fire in the bottom of a steep narrow canyon. Second, strong upcanyon winds pushing the fire up the canyon and upslope. Third, the fire burning into the green (not previously underburned) Gambel oak canopy." In summary, the report concluded that the area's topography—steep slopes and deep ravines—was the primary culprit, making visibility difficult, channeling intense wind gusts, and limiting escape routes for firefighters. The report further concluded, "The transition from a slow-spreading, low-intensity fire to a fast-moving, high-intensity fire occurs rapidly. This seems to surprise firefighters most often in live fuels." Though a federal investigator's report found that "just about everyone involved had been negligent in some way," another investigative team was more fatalistic, adopting the "preferred view that the West was apocalyptically dry" that summer and that "huge fires were bound to happen. On such fires, people sometimes die."

Fire in the Sky

The lightning that started the South Canyon fire was just one of approximately 25 million strikes that occur annually in the United States, though "flash density"—the number of lightning strikes per square kilometer per year—can vary tremendously from region to region and season to season. In the West, the Rocky Mountain states from Colorado south to New Mexico and west into Arizona show a flash density of four to eight strikes per square kilometer per year, whereas the flash density of coastal California is close to zero. Florida leads the nation in flash density with about ten strikes per kilometer annually, but since the storms that produce lightning in the intermountain West do not occur year-round (as they do in Florida), the rate of lightning strikes per storm can be considered nearly comparable.

The number of lightning fatalities for the years 1990 through 2003 appear to bear this out. Florida led the nation in lightning-caused deaths for the period with 126, followed by Texas with 52, and Colorado was third with 39 deaths. (The U.S. total was 756.) But looked at another way—fatality per million people—five of the Rocky Mountain states rank among the top six most dangerous places to be in a thunderstorm. Wyoming tops the list with 2.02 fatalities per million, followed by Utah with 0.7 and Colorado with 0.65. Florida ranks fourth with 0.56, closely followed by Montana and New Mexico with 0.55 each. The meteorologist who compiled the data, Ronald L. Holle, a consultant with weather instrument maker Vaisala, also noted "a continuing shift to the south and west in death rates caused by lightning." This makes perfect sense, since these are the parts of the country that have seen the greatest population growth in recent years.

Why so many storms? As discussed previously, heat, topography, and monsoonal moisture all combine in the summer months over the central-to-southern Rockies to create a volatile mix of wind, rain (or hail), thunder, and lightning. More specifically, the developmental sequence of a typical Rocky Mountain thunderstorm goes something like this: As increasing heat during the day warms the ground, air starts to rise, creating an updraft. As the air rises, it expands and cools, forming clouds. Soon ice crystals or water drops become too heavy to overcome the updraft, and start falling, pulling down cool air. The downdrafts eventually overcome the updrafts and the storm rains itself out. Most storms in the Rockies last no more than an hour, unless energized by a cold front or unusually high humidity levels. This region can see storms on at least sixty days per year, making it, in the eyes of one veteran meteorologist, "the thunderstorm capital of the United States."

A typical summer scene in the American West: rains fall as a thunderstorm builds over a mountain lake. (National Park Service, Yellowstone National Park; photo by Jim Peaco)

As the American Meteorological Society (AMS) cautions, a storm does not have to be directly overhead for it to provide a threat of lightning. Lightning can strike miles from a storm, well outside the area of rain, and even from smaller "debris" clouds well after a storm has moved off or seemingly dissipated.

Furthermore, "lightning does not 'decide' where it will strike until the stepped leader [lightning bolt] is about thirty meters" from what's about to be struck. Contrary to popular thinking, lightning doesn't necessarily seek the tallest nearby object, and can still be deadly more than a hundred feet away from the initial strike. As Richard Keen graphically explains in his essential book *Skywatch West: The Complete Weather Guide*, "The *instantaneous* peak rate of energy use may exceed a trillion watts, equivalent to the *average* consumption rate of the entire United States." This is no better illustrated, Keen explains, than observing the effect of lightning on what it strikes: in a fraction of a second it can melt sand at 3,100°F, creating glassy blobs called fulgurites.

Lightning deaths and injuries are so frequent in favored areas of the West because "many people tend to be outside precisely when the lightning hazard is at its greatest." The typical victim, based on statistical data, is predominantly a male who is outdoors between the hours of noon and 4 p.m. on a July afternoon. In 1997 NOAA reported that nationally for the years from 1959 to 1994, 84 percent of victims were male; 14 percent were seeking shelter under trees; 32 percent were caught out in open areas like fields or golf courses; and the most common days of the week for incidents to occur were Sunday, Wednesday, and Saturday, in that order. More than 3 percent of fatal incidents involved a telephone, radio, transmitter, or antenna.

Surprising, given these grim statistics, 90 percent of lightning-strike victims survive, but often suffer lifelong, debilitating injuries. Burns are the most obvious manifestation of a lightning strike, including burns received from clothing melting into skin. Electrical injuries to blood vessels can lead to hemorrhaging or thrombosis. Neurological damage includes lesions of the brain, degeneration of nerve ganglia, and intracranial bleeding; survivors of a lightning strike often suffer from memory loss, lack of sleep, and dizziness. The pressure of a thunder shock wave can rupture sensitive ear membranes, and a lightning flash can cause cataracts to develop in the eyes. Two-thirds of lightning victims suffer some sort of paralysis, mostly to the lower extremities.

The most obvious ways to avoid being struck by lightning are to always know the updated weather forecast and stay indoors if that forecast calls for lightning. However, if you are caught outdoors, the AMS recommends employing the "30-30 rule":

> When you see lightning, count the time until you hear thunder. If this time is 30 seconds or less, go immediately to a safer place. If you can't see the lightning, just hearing the thunder means lightning is likely within striking range. After the storm has apparently dissipated or moved on, wait 30 minutes or more before leaving the safer location.

The AMS describes a "safer location" as ideally "a large, fully enclosed, substantially constructed building," such as "your typical house, school, library, or other public building." However, once inside, stay away from anything that can conduct electricity, such as corded telephones, electrical appliances, and plumbing. If a "safer location" is not available, a car with a solid metal roof and metal doors makes a "reasonable second choice" (convertibles and cars with fiberglass or plastic shells do not).

Many victims of lightning strikes in the West are struck in the higher elevations of the mountains, where storms form quickly, early, and sometimes completely unexpectedly. (Indeed, one rule of thumb that climbers follow is "down by noon," to avoid inevitable early afternoon storms.) The most obvious course of action when a storm begins to form is to lose altitude quickly and try to get down below timberline, but failing that seek shelter behind or beneath a rock outcropping. On Colorado's 14,433-foot Mount Elbert on Sunday, August 12, 2007, Justin Eggleston and his girlfriend, Jamie Willett, were trying to do just that when lightning suddenly struck Eggleston in the head, knocking him unconscious. Fortunately, a doctor from Aspen witnessed the accident; he had been hastily descending the mountain as well. When Eggleston regained consciousness his muscles began to cramp, so the doctor, Willett, and other climbers in the vicinity had to help him down the mountain in an agonizing two-hour descent. Displaying classic after effects of a lightning strike, Eggleston could not feel his feet, hands, or lips, and though he could hear people talk, he couldn't respond. As the Boulder Daily Camera reported, however, after Eggleston was taken to the hospital "Paramedics checked his heart and brain and found no damage. But when they looked at the protein in his muscles, they found skyrocketing levels." Using his own error of judgment as example, his stern advice to fellow climbers was, "You should be coming down the mountain at noon, not summiting at three p.m. A storm can brew in seconds. Even if you see white clouds, don't take it lightly. It can be a serious matter."

Mighty Winds

Severe thunderstorms can also spawn tornadoes, and where and how they occur in the western United States can help us see past the myths that have come to be associated with these powerful phenomena. One of the most enduring myths is that tornadoes can't, and don't, form over mountains. In fact, tornadoes have been spotted in the mountains above 11,000 feet on at least two occasions; crossing a section of Long's Peak on August 17, 1984, and touching down near Rockwell Pass in Sequoia National Park on July 7, 2004. Though the record is unofficial, the Rockwell Pass tornado is claimed to be the highest ever observed at 11,600 feet.

Fujita Tornado Damage Scale
Developed in 1971 by T. Theodore Fujita of the University of Chicago

SCALE	WIND ESTIMATE *** (MPH)	TYPICAL DAMAGE
F0	< 73	**Light damage.** Some damage to chimneys; branches broken off trees; shallow-rooted trees pushed over; sign boards damaged.
F1	73–112	**Moderate damage.** Peels surface off roofs; mobile homes pushed off foundations or overturned; moving autos blown off roads
F2	113–157	**Considerable damage.** Roofs torn off frame houses; mobile homes demolished; boxcars overturned; large trees snapped or uprooted; light-object missiles generated; cars lifted off ground.
F3	158–206	**Severe damage.** Roofs and some walls torn off well-constructed houses; trains overturned; most trees in forest uprooted; heavy cars lifted off the ground and thrown.
F4	207–260	**Devastating damage.** Well-constructed houses leveled; structures with weak foundations blown away some distance; cars thrown and large missiles generated.
F5	261–318	**Incredible damage.** Strong frame houses leveled off foundations and swept away; automobile-size missiles fly through the air in excess of 100 meters (109 yards); trees debarked; incredible phenomena will occur.

Source: NOAA website.

By far the most spectacular mountain tornado to ever occur touched down in the Teton-Yellowstone area on July 21, 1987, cutting a swath through the forest a mile and a half wide and over twenty-four miles long. An estimated 1 million trees in a thirty-six-square-mile area were either uprooted or knocked down in what investigators described as "a most unlikely place . . . where a tornado of this intensity would not be expected to occur." The tornado initially touched down as an F1 (see table), then grew in intensity as it moved northeastward. Its first obstacle was 8,858-foot Gravel Ridge, where it caused considerable damage on the ridge's northeast or downslope side. It then moved over Enos Lake and Pacific Creek Valley, continuing to flatten the forest, then passed over the Continental Divide at above 10,000 feet, damaging trees inside three glacial cirques. Though witnesses reported seeing no funnel cloud, they did report hearing "a roar like a train in the distance." Once over the Yellowstone River Valley, the storm began to weaken and dissipate. Still, the tornado's confirmed F4 damage was "an intensity rarely experienced in the Rockies." Ironically, the Yellowstone fires of 1988 burned through much of the devastated woodland, curtailing the efforts of researchers and scientists to engage in long-term studies of such massive blow-downs.

Though one can only imagine the large number of animals that probably perished in the Teton–Yellowstone tornado, no human deaths or injuries were recorded because the tornado just happened to touch down in a remote section of the greater Yellowstone ecosystem. Had it formed perhaps twenty miles to the north and west, it might have ranked as one of the greatest natural disasters of our time, clogging the West Thumb Geyser Basin with debris, causing severe damage to the structures at popular Grant Village, blocking one of the main routes into the park with thousands of downed trees, and possibly injuring or killing scores of people at the height of Yellowstone's tourist season. Because so few people were affected by this highly unusual phenomenon, however, interest was limited to a handful of meteorologists and foresters.

Tornadoes are capricious, though, and can strike anywhere in the world anytime. (In 1976, a tornado even touched down above the arctic circle in Alaska.) The state of Utah records an average of only two tornadoes annually, but one that occurred on August 11, 1999, managed to single out Salt Lake City among the state's 84,904 mostly vacant square miles, debunking another myth—tornadoes can't occur in cities.

The Salt Lake City tornado dropped from the sky at about 1 p.m. right over downtown, uprooting trees, destroying thirty-four homes and countless cars, and damaging the roof of the twenty-thousand-seat Delta Center. A temporary pavilion set up for an outdoor retailers convention was ripped apart "as if the structure was tissue paper," killing Allen Crandy, thirty-eight, when a metal beam collapsed on him. Fortunately, Crandy was the tornado's only fatality, though a hundred people were sent to hospitals with injuries, a dozen of them serious. Given the tornado's path right through downtown, the outcome could have been much worse. Although it caused more than $100 million in damages, it managed to bypass such landmarks as the Mormon Temple, the Utah Capitol, and the Union Pacific train station.

Tornadoes become more frequent just east of the Rockies, culminating in Colorado's very own contribution to "tornado alley" on its high eastern plains. Though tornadoes in the West aren't nearly as big (on average) as their eastern counterparts, their frequency in certain areas can actually be greater. One particular "hot spot" is in the northeast corner of Colorado, where up to 1.8 tornadoes per twenty-five square miles can occur annually. This compares to an average of 1.4 tornadoes per twenty-five square miles in Oklahoma and Texas. Given the modest size and comparative brevity of a "Front Range" tornado, a direct hit on a town or city is rare, but this doesn't mean it won't be any less devastating than other tornadoes. Cheyenne, Wyoming, over the border from Colorado, was struck by two tornadoes (one an F3) on July 16, 1979, destroying more than 150 homes. Three tornadoes raced across the northern suburbs of Denver on June 3, 1981, destroying 87 homes in the city of Thornton. And on June 6, 1990, most of downtown Limon, Colorado, was destroyed by an unusually powerful tornado that displaced 177 families, injured 14 people, and caused $12 million in damages.

The tornado season in eastern Colorado generally begins in late spring and peaks in June, roughly two months later than the Midwest. Nevertheless, nature pays no attention to the calendar, so when a fierce tornado hit the town of Holly, Colorado, on March 28, the town's one thousand residents were not the only ones surprised: so were weather forecasters. Although a tornado watch had been posted that evening for extreme western Kansas—Holly is four miles from its border—the National Weather Service in Pueblo decided not to issue a similar watch for Colorado because dry, stable air had started to push across the area and into Kansas. However, the storm in Kansas suddenly doubled back into Colorado and spawned the tornado that slammed into Holly just before 8 p.m. The weather service issued a tornado warning literally as the funnel cloud was touching down, allowing no time to activate Holly's warning siren. The tornado cut a six-hundred-foot-wide swath of destruction directly through the town, destroying thirty-five homes and damaging thirty-two others, sending seven people to local hospitals and causing Colorado's first tornado fatality in forty-seven years. Making matters worse, Holly had just emerged from eastern Colorado's challenging winter of 2006–2007, when a succession of blizzards caused widespread losses of livestock.

Powerful, straight-line winds are also a feature of the climate of the American West, and their legendary status has been no better exemplified than by the names that have been attached to them over the years, such as Chinook and Santa Ana.

Chinooks (derived from the Indian word for "snow-eater") are perhaps the most widespread of western winds, occurring mostly on the lee side of north–south running mountain ranges such as the Sierra, Cascades, and Rockies. Often propelled by the jet stream far above, the very compression of the winds as they are pushed downslope has a warming effect that can flip temperatures tens of degrees upward in a matter of minutes during the winter months (the time most Chinooks occur). Thus on the east slopes of the Rockies snow can melt rapidly with the arrival of a Chinook; a common snow pattern in midwinter viewed from high above the Rockies, for example, would show snow-covered mountains to the west, a brown band of dry ground along and to the east of the foothills, followed by a resumption of snow cover on the eastern plains where the effect of a Chinook dissipates.

The downside to a Chinook is its ability to produce hurricane-force winds. Normally salubrious and trendy Boulder, Colorado, by virtue of its proximity to the Continental Divide and bowl-shaped valley where the foothills meet the plains, "has some of the highest peak winds of any city in the U.S.," according to a NOAA publication. On average, Boulder experiences more than twenty wind "events" in excess of 90 miles per hour in a typical December, nearly twenty such events in January, and ten plus in February. For half of the years from 1966 to 2002, Boulder recorded a wind gust in excess of 100 miles per hour. Boulder's highest recorded wind gust occurred at, appropriately, the National Center for Atmospheric Research, where on January 23, 1971, a gust was clocked at 147 miles per hour. Such winds can, of course, be incredibly destructive. A windstorm that occurred on January 16–17, 1982, damaged 40 percent of all structures in Boulder and toppled power poles. House trailers were knocked over by 115-mile-per-hour winds on December 7, 1977, which blew all day.

Rare but certainly possible, damaging windstorms can occur anytime of year along and east of the Rockies. On June 8, 2007, a powerful winterlike storm that brought rain, snow, and even tornadoes to southern Wyoming dragged winds in excess of 100 miles per hour across the mountains and foothills of Colorado, causing widespread power outages in several Front Range cities and damaging thousands of trees and dozens of cars. The damage was perhaps greater than that of a winter windstorm of equal magnitude because trees had fully leafed out, leaves acting as sails on fragile spars. One unlucky couple in Boulder lost not only a century-old maple tree but also two cars the tree had fallen onto. (The authors, residents of the east Boulder County city of Lafayette, were vacationing in Connecticut that week, but had unwisely assembled their canvas-topped gazebo just before they left. When they returned on June 10, they found the remains of the gazebo a twisted tower of metal with shredded canvas pathetically flapping in the breeze like so many weather-beaten flags.)

Similar to a Chinook in its dynamics but blowing in the opposite direction, a typical Santa Ana wind is created when high pressure builds over the Great Basin in autumn or winter, causing cold air to sink and push westward over California's San Gabriel, San Bernardino, and Santa Ana mountains. As the air is forced downslope toward the Los Angeles Basin and other coastal cities, compression warms the air at a rate of about 29°F per mile of descent. The desiccating wind gathers further velocity as it winds through passes and canyons. Although Santa Anas seldom approach the speed of a Chinook—25 to 35 miles per hour is the norm, with some gusts as high as 70 miles per hour—the dry, hot winds quickly reduce the moisture in the drought-tolerant chaparral that covers the hills of Southern California, setting the stage for fires of biblical proportions. And it has ever been thus: charcoal records reveal the frequency of wildfires in Southern California has not changed measurably in five hundred years, notwithstanding the arrival of millions of potential fire-starters beginning in the mid-nineteenth century as white settlement began.

Santa Ana winds fueled the largest and perhaps deadliest fire in California history, when from October 25 to November 2, 2003, what became known as the Cedar Fire burned more than 280,000 acres in central San Diego County, destroying nearly three thousand buildings and killing fifteen people. Part of a series of fires kicked up by Santa Anas that would eventually burn nearly 750,000 acres in six counties, the Cedar Fire began in the Cleveland National Forest when lost hunter Sergio Martinez started a fire to signal a rescue helicopter. Within hours, winds had pushed the fire down Wildcat Canyon, amid a cluster of homes southeast of Escondido, also cutting off the only escape route through the nearby San Vicente Indian Reservation. Subjected to "two hours of terror and panic," twelve people died either in their homes or while trying to escape; some burned to death in their cars. The only firefighter fatality occurred a few days later when Steven Rucker, a firefighter from Novato, California, perished while trying to save a home.

A more debatable hazard associated with Santa Ana winds is that they possess "a greater number of positive ions" than stable air "and are blamed for sudden rises in traffic accidents, rioting, depression, suicide, murder, and poor decision-making in Hollywood." Although verification can't be found anywhere in serious anthropological studies, a myth carried down over the years claims that Southern California's Indians threw themselves into the sea during intense Santa Anas. (Perhaps they were just escaping fire.) The supposed negative psychological influences of the winds have found their way into literature over the years, further adding to their reputation. In his short story "The Red Wind," Raymond Chandler wrote that Santa Anas "come down through the mountain passes and curl your hair and make your nerves jump. . . . On nights like that every booze party ends in a fight. Meek little wives feel the edge of the carving knife and study their husband's necks." In an essay titled "Santa Ana" from her book *Slouching Toward Bethlehem,* Joan Didion describes more mundane behaviors associated with the winds: "The baby frets. The maid sulks. I rekindle a waning argument with the telephone company, then cut my losses and lie down, given over to whatever it is in the air."

Winds of Change?

For all its periodic ferocity, weather in the West can be placid and salubrious for extended periods of time. A Santa Ana day, for example, is offset by many more days in which, as the saying goes, there is "no weather at all"—endless sunshine, moderate temperatures, and no precipitation in sight. The mountain states in particular experience a "shoulder" or "fifth" season from roughly late August to early October, where days are warm, nights are cool, storms are few, and changing aspen leaves flutter in the breeze against an impossibly blue, cloudless sky. Indeed, this is why many of us moved here, weighing those three hundred sunny, dry days against five dozen days of inclement weather.

But will it last? The fact is, no one really knows, and anyone who claims that he or she knows with any certainty is "charitably misinformed, or chooses to be," according to one scientist who has studied climate history since 1995. It's a sad statement of where the current climate debate stands that the words "climate change" have become a pejorative expression, since the climate is always changing and we don't even know what an optimal climate is. Perhaps it is now; perhaps it was during the so-called Medieval Warm Period, from roughly AD 900–1300 when Greenland experienced enough ice melt to support agriculture. But was that warming optimal for the arid, drought-sensitive American West? Is colder better for humans, wildlife, and ecosystems in general? What additional dangers, if any, will climate change bring in either direction? Since we have been taken by surprise many times in trying to second-guess nature—recall the wildlife biologist Maurice Hornocker's statement (see "Rampant Lion: The Cougar") that fifty years ago he "would never have dreamed of the number of encounters between lions and people we see now"—all we have are the paleoclimatic record and any number of sophisticated but highly speculative computer models to go by.

Still, this has not stopped scientists and nonscientists alike from making sometimes bold prognostications about the effects on the western landscape of climate change, mostly of the warm variety. A report titled *Losing Ground: Western National Parks Endangered by Climate Disruption* issued by the Rocky Mountain Climate Organization and the National Resources Defense Council in 2006 opens with the statement that "A climate disrupted by human activities poses such sweeping threats to the scenery, natural and cultural resources, and wildlife of the West's national parks that dwarfs all previous risks to these American treasures." If you look at the "threats," however, you can also interpret them as perfectly natural responses to natural climate change—otherwise known as adaptations. Indeed, the report was written with barely a nod to previous warm, dry periods, as if the current warming was an anomaly. And in an awkward attempt to make climate change relevant to the average citizen, the report doesn't help itself with such tortured statements as "Unnatural increases in wildfires can disrupt summer vacations" and "Americans will have fewer opportunities to enjoy the magic of a snow-covered Yellowstone National Park or other western national parks."

What we know from both the historic and paleoclimatic record is that periods of warming have occurred before, and that we have a marvelous record of the precise dangers they have posed to humans and animals alike. In other words, we have a general idea of what to expect. While the Medieval Warm Period was good for Europe, it also caused persistent drought in the American Southwest, leading to water shortages and crop failures. For the Chumash Indians of Southern California, though, warming also coincided with a deep-water upwelling in coastal waters, "making local fisheries extremely productive," in the words of one prominent anthropologist. Indeed, drought seems to be the rule rather than the exception in the American Southwest, since "tree-ring records show that the high rainfall totals of the mid-twentieth century occurred only three times in this thousand-year tree-ring record." There is no question that the American West is susceptible to warm periods and drought— after all, parts of it have been called the "Great American Desert"— but it's also true that humans have found a way to adapt to it, if uncomfortably, and often in spite of it. From 1849 to 1905, for example, Arizona experienced severe, persistent drought, but during that same time it was settled and became a U.S. territory.

A recent study of precipitation in Yellowstone from AD 1173 to 1998 shows that even in the northern Rockies periods of drought-producing warmth are nothing new. Published in the journal *Quaternary Research*, the study of the tree rings of 133 limber pines and Douglas fir found "extreme wet and dry years within the instrumental period fall within the range of past variability." Furthermore, "the magnitude of the worst-case droughts of the 20th century (AD 1930s and 1950s) was likely equaled or exceeded at least thirty times in the preceding six centuries." And in a conclusion that could have described conditions just prior to the Yellowstone fires of 1988, the scientists described historical "high amplitude switching between persistent wet and dry conditions." Interestingly, the goal of the study was to determine if present warming was an anomaly. Not only did they find it wasn't, but the drought cycles correlated with other data gathered both regionally and from around the world.

Another benchmark of climate change is advancing or retreating glaciers and snow-pack levels, the variability of which poses dangers at both extremes. Vanishing glaciers and low snow-pack levels can disrupt water supplies to already drought-stricken cities; too much snow can aid and abet flash flooding when it thaws in late spring. Confusing matters is that global warming is often used to explain both phenomena. Although we expect glaciers to be retreating as Earth proceeds further into a warming interglacial period, not all such ice sheets are participating. *Losing Ground*, for example, details glacial retreat in Glacier, North Cascades, Mount Rainier, Olympic, and Yosemite national parks, but notably leaves out three prominent alpine ecosystems where glaciers are advancing or stable: Rocky Mountain and Grand Teton national parks, and California's Mount Shasta. Shasta, in fact, has provided a dra-

A view of Rocky Mountain National Park, showing a few of its many glaciers. Notwithstanding estimates of global warming of approximately one degree Fahrenheit over the last hundred years, glaciers are generally holding
steady or expanding in the park. (National Park Service, Rocky Mountain National Park)

matic example of glacial growth, with Whitney Glacier alone now
larger than it was in 1890. Evidently this, too, can be attributed to
global warming; some scientists believe that warmer air contains
more moisture, piling on snow at higher elevations. Others take a
somewhat more agnostic view of the expanding glacier conundrum:
after geologists compared existing glaciers in Rocky Mountain National Park during the summer of 2001with historical photos, finding that some glaciers had expanded—they also discovered a hundred
new glaciers in their survey—park spokeswoman Judy Visty admitted, "We're not quite in synch with global warming here."

Equally inconclusive is what effect climate change will have on
wildlife populations, since it may be difficult to differentiate a "natural" adaptation to a warmer or cooler climate from adaptations
as a result of habitat loss, human interference with wildlife corridors, or the disappearance or reintroduction of predator species. As
discussed in the beginning of the book, the recent decline of the elk
population in Yellowstone has been variously attributed to drought,
wolf reintroduction, or some combination of both. Wild animals are

also affected by changes in the foods upon which they depend. Whitebark pine seeds, for example, are a vital part of the grizzly bear's diet as it approaches denning in the fall, but a combination of factors has conspired to devastate whitebark pine trees throughout the west: fire; blister rust, an exotic fungus accidentally introduced from Europe in about 1910; and pine beetles, which invade and kill the high-altitude trees during periods of warmth. Although grizzlies have survived periodic shortages of whitebark pine seeds in the past, the concern is that the current scarcity of seeds will force grizzlies to consider alternatives that will put them in conflict with humans. Still, there is no evidence that we can expect an epidemic of grizzly attacks as a result of the decline of the whitebark pine alone.

Although admitting there are "only a few studies of the vulnerability of species in particular national parks," the authors of *Losing Ground* nevertheless make the claim that "more than 80 percent of species showing changes in their ranges are changing in directions consistent with climate change." Well, we should hope so. Since climate isn't static, why should an ecosystem be? The authors also suggest that some species could become "locally extinct," a rather grave condemnation of animals that may have simply moved on to better habitat. Equally puzzling is the authors' apparent alarm that climate change "accelerates the spread of non-native animals that pose threats to native wildlife." Never mind that yesterday's "locally extinct" species is likely to become today's "invasive" species in somebody's ecosystem.

Nevertheless, short-term climate change does have consequences that we can't always anticipate, and that perhaps we can only manage. The recent warm winters in Alberta, Canada, for example, have caused deer, elk, and moose populations to increase and expand their ranges at the same time that municipalities have expanded onto their habitat. The proximity of ungulates to human communities has had the consequence of bringing their primary predator, cougars, into closer contact with people, resulting in a dramatic increase in the number of sightings of the cat in the province from 2005 to 2007. Still, a scientist monitoring Alberta's cougars described the fluctuating ungulate populations as "natural," suggesting they will also ebb in cooler winters, perhaps taking the cougars with them.

If a warmer climate has the effect, among others, of emboldening the West's two deadliest predators a bit, what would be the consequences of a cooler climate? We really don't know, because research dollars are currently being wagered on forecasting what will happen to us in a warmer world. However, abrupt cooling is not only possible but probable at some point in the future, and one need only look to a sleeping giant in the northwest corner of Wyoming to understand why.

Yellowstone National Park sits on top of one of the world's "hot spots," an area of intense volcanic activity responsible for many of the park's geysers and other thermal features. Three so-called supervolcanoes 2,500 times the size of the 1980 Mount Saint Helens eruption have occurred on the Yellowstone plateau over the past 2.1 million years, the most recent of which created a massive caldera

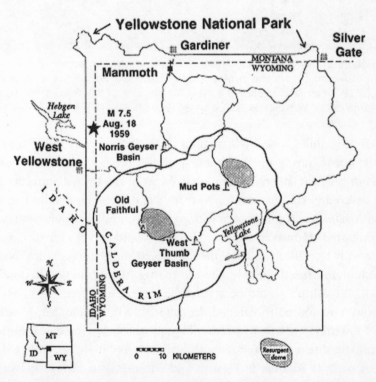

A map of Yellowstone, showing the location of its huge supervolcanic caldera. (National Park Service, Yellowstone National Park)

Members of the Washington National Guard identifying victims of the eruption of Mount St. Helens in May 1980. This could be the scene in places
as far south as Arizona should a full-scale eruption of the Yellowstone super-
volcano occur. (National Park Service, Mt. St. Helens National Park; photo by Ralph Perry)

thirty-five miles wide by fifty miles long. Should an eruption on this
scale occur during our lifetimes, scientists predict the effects would
be not only catastrophic but global. Most of the United States would
be covered in volcanic ash (up to three feet thick as far south as northern Arizona) and much of Wyoming, Idaho, and Montana would be
obliterated. However, because the ash would travel globally in the
atmosphere, reflecting back the sun's heat and trumping any possible human-caused agent of climate change, the world would quickly
cool, agriculture would be severely curtailed, and civilization as we
know it would be threatened. In other words, "game, set, match."

How likely is this to occur? Though the U.S. Geological Survey
rates the threat of a Yellowstone eruption as "high"—active volcanoes such as Kilauea in Hawaii and Mount Saint Helens in Washington are rated as "very high" threats, by way of comparison—it
also states that "the Yellowstone volcanic system shows no signs that

it is headed toward such an eruption. The probability of a large caldera-forming eruption within the next few thousand years is exceedingly low." The USGS further puts the odds of a Yellowstone eruption anytime soon on par with the likelihood that an asteroid will strike Earth during our lifetime. (Perhaps this is not that great a comfort, though: a massive explosion in Siberia in 1908 has been attributed by many to have been created by an asteroid impact, and some scientists are even predicting another asteroid will strike Earth as early as 2035.) Still, since caldera-forming (that is, massive) eruptions seem to occur every 640,000 years or so in the Yellowstone region, and that the last one occurred about 640,000 years or so, we may be due. Fortunately, such estimates have margins of error of several tens of thousands of years, so the danger is probably not imminent.

As long as the Yellowstone plateau remains docile for the foreseeable future, it will also serve as an example of the balance we have achieved in preserving large areas of the western landscape without compromising the economic vitality of adjacent communities. The question now is how growth can continue to be managed so as not to compromise the very principles of conservation that attract people in the first place. Recognition and preservation of wildlife corridors is a good start, as well as taking steps to avoid conflict between wild animals and humans. As a recent report by an advocacy group concludes with regard to Yellowstone, "A focused, regional effort will be essential to directing the momentum of growth and protecting the long-term health of these natural assets. Business, community, and government leadership will be indispensable in building the broad commitment and new collaboration from which this investment—in time, vision, and money—will come."

VIII

Wild Still:
Two Weeks in September

As we were wrapping up work on this book, a fortnight of news stories came to crystallize a number of topics discussed in the preceding seven chapters, from increasing wild animal encounters to the mysterious disappearance of an American hero in the vastness of Nevada's Great Basin. While the following events from September 1 to 14, 2007, are not necessarily unusual for a wild expanse like the American West—take a similar snapshot at any time of year, and you will find ever more examples of the dominance of nature in our everyday lives—they do provide some perspective. For just as the absence of a sense of history will trivialize an interpretation of current events, the lack of a sense of scale can give us an inordinate sense of our importance to the world around us.

On September 1, 2007, Southern California entered its second day of what would turn out to be a weeklong heat wave, with temperatures as high as 112°F in the Woodland Hills section of Los Angeles. An estimated twenty-eight people died from the intense heat, mostly elderly whose homes lacked air conditioning. However, one of the victims was a twenty-six-year-old dirt biker who had succumbed to the heat after being separated from friends north of Los Angeles. By the afternoon of September 6, temperatures had finally eased back into the 80s, but a thousand Southern California Edison customers were still without power.

* * *

Also on September 1, Terry Jones—fifty-six, and his wife Marion—49, were dropped off by their son at the Chapin Pass trailhead in Rocky Mountain National Park for a brief, overnight campout roughly seven miles down the trail. They had planned to hike out of the park the following day via the Big South trailhead along Colorado 14, where their car awaited. When they didn't return Sunday night, authorities were notified and sixty people began a search for the couple. After four days of searching, a Civil Air Patrol airplane saw smoke coming from a ridge above the Poudre River and Terry frantically waving a white T-shirt. A yellow Lab search-and-rescue dog named Loki then led rescuers to the couple, who were still fit enough to walk out on their own. The well-equipped Joneses had benefited from their backcountry experience, exceptionally good weather, and generally good spirits. "We each lost it at times but we both never lost it at the same time," Terry recalled, saying that the low point for them had come the day before they were found, when a helicopter had actually flown beneath them as they waved undetected from a ridge at nine thousand feet. "He's the right man to get lost with," Marion said of her husband. "I always asked him why he brings so much stuff but we used everything."

With days getting shorter and nights cooler, wildlife was on the move in Boulder County, Colorado, in early September 2007. On the morning of September 2, Otsie Stowell of Nederland had found the remains of his four-hundred-pound miniature horse "Bodacious," clearly the work of a mountain lion. The lion reappeared the following day to eat more of the horse, then returned again on September 4, when it sat in the grass and stared at Stowell. By this time, Stowell had had enough and called wildlife officials. "My other horses are wound pretty tight right now," he said. "This cat feels pretty comfortable around people and the area that I live in." When a spokesperson for the northeastern region of the state Division of Wildlife announced that the cat would be trapped and euthanized, however, a conflicted public clogged the blogosphere with a fury more typical of a starlet scandal than a wild animal attack.

The first salvo was fired by a wildlife conservation organization known as Sinapu, which immediately objected to the death sentence. Wendy Keefover-Ring, director of Sinapu's Carnivore Protection Program, stated, "With shrinking habitats and an increased human population in Boulder County, we need to expand people's knowledge and change behaviors if large carnivores such as lions and bears are to persist. I usually remain silent when the Colorado Division of Wildlife has to kill a mountain lion or a bear for human safety, but in this instance . . . the lion should not have to pay for the livestock grower's mistake with his/her life."

Comments posted at the end of a *Daily Camera* online article about the attack mostly expressed agreement with Sinapu, ranging from a brief "*Please* don't kill the lion" to a shot at Stowell for keeping his horses out at night: "Maybe you should move to Westminster where they already killed the wildlife." There were the usual poor attempts at humor, such as "Toy horse = lion entrée" and "Relocate the lion deeper into the mountains and relocate the [horse] owner back to Denver," but a number of contributors to the lengthy string of comments admitted the issue was not at all clear-cut. Wrote one, "These stories seem to prompt people to say we are living in the lion's territory (or bear's, wolf's, etc.). Where exactly is human territory? Anywhere a human lives will be in some other specie's territory. I don't want this animal killed . . . but I don't necessarily think the lion owns this territory."

A similar controversy arose when a large black bear refused to move from atop a tree in a Boulder neighborhood on the morning of September 10. Nearby Fairview High School was locked down for two hours while wildlife officials tried to encourage the bear out of the tree by blasting it with a hose, both responses to the presence of the rogue bruin coming under fire from animal welfare activists and public safety officials alike. Fairview administrators defended their decision to lock down the school (though the bear was still in the tree when the lockdown was lifted), while some citizens who espoused a "live and let live" philosophy thought the move was overly cautious. As it happens, the bear disappeared into the foothills that night, only to reappear in another part of the city the following Friday. With a growing "rap" sheet—the bear had been caught, tagged, and relocated once before—wildlife officers made the decision to euthanize the animal while members of the Boulder City Council openly discussed new laws designed to protect both bears and humans.

On Friday, September 14, bow hunter Dustin Flack was calling for elk near Yellowstone National Park when he noticed a sow grizzly with cubs twenty-five yards away, heading in his direction. Although the bears didn't appear to notice him at first, his attempt to hide behind an eight-inch-diameter tree didn't fool the sow, and he was forced to climb the small tree. But the bear stood up on its hind legs and bit Flack on his toes, shin, and calf before "She ripped the tree in half and pulled me down with it," as the hunter recalled. Flack then curled up in the fetal position and put his hands behind his neck, but after biting or clawing his back the sow seemed to lose interest and wandered away with her cubs. Flack remained on the ground for about five minutes, then climbed a tree and stayed there for another fifteen minutes to make sure the coast was clear. After tying up his leg to slow the bleeding, he hiked out two miles to a road, where a good samaritan picked him up, took him to his car, and called an ambulance. Officials closed areas in and near Yellowstone National Park following the attack, but decided to take no action against the bear. "She was doing what sows do, which is protect their cubs," said an official with the Montana Department of Fish, Wildlife and Parks.

By mid-September Dr. Bruce Parks, a medical examiner in Pima County, Arizona, had tallied a record 181 heat-related deaths of illegal immigrants attempting to cross the Arizona border for the period from January 1 to September 8. The previous record for that period had been established in 2005, with 166 recorded deaths. However, Border Patrol officials maintained that the increased number of recovered bodies in 2007 was a consequence of having more agents available to patrol the border than in previous years. "The patrol doesn't want to see any deaths," said a spokeswoman for the patrol's Tucson sector. "Our ideal would be that there would be none. The positive is that our rescue numbers are high."

*   *   *

On the crystal-clear morning of September 1, 2007, famed adventurer Steve Fossett took off from a private airfield eighty miles southeast of Reno, Nevada, for what was supposed to be a three-hour joy ride in a single-engine Champion Citabria. He was never seen again.

Fossett, a veteran pilot famous for becoming the first person to complete a solo, nonstop circumnavigation of Earth in a balloon as well as the longest nonstop flight in aviation history, did not file a flight plan and apparently was not wearing a special wristwatch that allowed him to signal his location. The Citabria did have an emergency locator transponder (ELT) that is automatically activated in the event of a crash, or by the pilot himself if need be, but for whatever reason searchers failed to detect a signal as more than a dozen aircraft took to the skies to look for Fossett. Ultimately covering an area of bleak, high desert the size of Massachusetts, the searchers came across six other plane wrecks, a number of them previously unreported, but none of them the Citabria.

As the search entered its twelfth day, family and friends dismissed the notion that Fossett's disappearance may have been deliberate, or that he had met with foul play. Neither his cell phone nor his credit cards had been used, nor had anyone reported seeing him. Ultimately, those involved in the search came to the conclusion that the landscape had not only overwhelmed Fossett and the Citabria, but also the modern technology that was employed to find him as well. Civil Air Patrol major Cynthia Ryan said the ELT might have been working just fine, "But when you've got terrain like we have here, line-of-sight issues, bouncing off canyon walls and not getting out, then you seriously diminish the ability of technology to do what it was designed to do." Furthermore, the ELT wouldn't have been effective if the plane had crashed into a lake and sunk.

Still, searchers had other technologies available to them to find Fosset, among them a new reconnaissance device named ARCHER that can analyze fifty light bands. (The human eye can detect only three.) National Guard aircraft equipped with forward-looking radar also joined in the search, and even amateur volunteers examined high resolution images of the Nevada landscape on Google and other websites. Still, the land seemed to have prevailed. "We've got 2007 technology . . . that can count beer cans in the back of a pickup," said Lyon County undersheriff Joe Sanford, "but we haven't found an airplane. That's frustrating."

Sources

Introduction

"Father's Effort to Save His Family Called 'Superhuman,'" CNN.com, December 7, 2006; Robert Adams, *Denver: A Photographic Survey of the Metropolitan Area* (Boulder: Colorado Associated University Press, 1977).

I. Theirs Is the Kingdom: Animal Attacks

For grizzly bear recovery announcement, U.S. Fish and Wildlife Service press release dated March 22, 2007; coyote in Central Park, James Barron, "A Coyote Leads a Crowd on a Central Park Marathon," *New York Times*, March 23, 2006.

Cute, Endearing, and Occasionally Deadly: The Black Bear–Robert Jordan, "Threat Behavior of the Black Bear (*Ursus Americanus*)," reprinted in Stephen Herrero, *Bear Attacks* (New York: Nick Lyons Books, 1983); *Bear Attacks*, pp. 105, 106, 108, and 115; Chase Squires, "Bear Encounters Increase Across the West," *Denver Post*, July 25, 2006; Tad Walch, Sara Israelsen, and Elizabeth Stuart, "Bear Blamed for Boy's Death in American Fork Canyon Is Killed," *Deseret Morning News*, June 19, 2007.

The American King of Beasts: The Grizzly Bear–Harold McCracken, *The Beast That Walks Like Man: the Story of the Grizzly Bear* (New York:

Doubleday, 1955); Paul Schullery, *The Bears of Yellowstone* (Boulder: Roberts Rinehart Publishers, 1986), pp. 65, 77–136; *Bear Attacks*, pp. 65, 70, 73; U.S. Department of the Interior, National Park Service, Yellowstone National Park, "Draft Report on Case Incident no. 842913, Brigitta Fredenhagen, July 30, 1984"; Sharon Anderson, "Racine Investigates Grizzly Mauling," *Glacier Reporter*, June 11, 1998; for attack on Jenna and John Otter, Associated Press, *Billings Gazette*, September 10, 2005; Glacier National Park website, "If You Encounter a Bear."

Rampant Lion: The Cougar–Harold P. Danz, *Cougar!* (Athens, Ohio: Swallow Press/Ohio University Press, 1999), pp. 88, 147, 161, 195; John Ennslin, and Gary Gebhardt, "Carcass Reveals Bone, Hair Tests on Mountain Lion Seek to Explain Attack," *Rocky Mountain News*, January 18, 1991; Angela Watercutter, "Bicyclist Mauled by Mountain Lion in Southern California," *San Diego Union-Tribune*, January 9, 2004; David Baron, "Wild in the Suburbs," *The Boston Globe Magazine*, August 22, 1999; Gary Gebhardt, "Experts Study Lion Attack Odds," *Rocky Mountain News*, April 25, 1991; David Baron, *The Beast in the Garden: A Modern Parable of Man and Nature* (New York: W.W. Norton and Company, 2004), p. 237, 239; *www.nps.gov/ccso/cougar.htm* for what to do in the event of a cougar attack.

Canidae–Scott Sandsberry, "Deadly Wolf Attacks Remain Rare in North America," *Yakima Herald Online*, January 18, 2007; Douglas W. Smith, and Gary Ferguson, *Decade of the Wolf: Returning the Wild to Yellowstone* (Guilford, CT: The Lyons Press, 2005), pp. 105–106; Robert M. Timm, Rex O. Baker, Joe R. Bennet, and Craig C. Coolahan, "Coyote Attacks: An Increasing Urban Problem," Proceedings of the 21st Vertebrate Pest Conference, University of California, Davis, 2004; Jan Klunder, "Child's Death Confirms Officials Fears About Coyotes," *Los Angeles Times*, August 30, 1981; *The Beast in the Garden*, p. 239.

Antlers, Hooves, and Bad Tempers–For figures on automobile/deer accidents, Insurance Institute for Highway Safety *Status Report*, Vol. 40, No. 1, January 3, 2005; Nick Gevock, "Deer Attacks Man in Madison Valley," *Bozeman Chronicle*, August 11, 2004; Mike Stark, "Park

Cuts off Elk's Antlers After Attacks," *Billings Gazette*, September 23, 2004; AP, "Aggressive Bull Moose Attacks Three Snowshoers," *Casper Star Tribune*, March 4, 2004; "Formal Study Reveals Extent of Bison Danger to Humans," *Billings Gazette*, April 18, 2000; Sebastian Junger, "Colter's Way," in *Fire* (New York: Perennial, 2002), pp. 147–153; *The Beast in the Garden*, pp. 225–226.

II. MISSING

For quotes on the vastness of the west: John G. Mitchell, "To the Edge of Forever," in *The World of Wilderness: Essays on the Power and Purpose of Wild Country* (Boulder: Roberts Rinehart Publishers in Cooperation with the Wilderness Society, 1997), p. 199; Charles R. Farabee, *Death, Daring, and Disaster: Search and Rescue in the National Parks* (Lanham, MD: Taylor Trade Publishing, 2005), p. 375.

Laura–Paul Ciotti, "Mike Bradbury's Obsession," *Los Angeles Times Magazine*, July 20, 1986; Carla Rivera, "Laura Bradbury Death Shown by DNA Evidence," *Los Angeles Times*, December 16, 1989.

The Iceman–Naomi Tward, "On the Rink of Success: NHL Draft Choice Eric LeMarque Bids to Catch on with Bruins," *Los Angeles Times*, February 2, 1990; Hector Becerra, and Steve Hymon, "Snowboarder Describes Days on Edge of Survival," *Los Angeles Times*, March 4, 2004; Andrew Murr, MCNBC/Newsweek Web Exclusive, March 16, 2004.

Missing: Deliberately–Hal Mansfield, "Manhunt," *Crime Magazine* online, June 3, 2000; Nancy Lofholm, and Electa Draper, "Cortez Police Officer Fatally Shot," *Denver Post*, May 30, 1998; Uncredited, "Massive Search Continues for Cop Killers," *San Juan Record*, June 3, 1998; Mark Eddy, "Fugitives Possess Skills for Survival," *Denver Post*, June 14, 1998; Carol Whitaker, "The Siege at Bluff," private diary entry, 1998; Electa Draper, "Affadavits Give Details in Manhunt," *Denver Post*, June 20, 1998; Kit Miniclier, "Massive Manhunt Scaled Way Back," *Denver Post*, June 8, 1998; Electa Draper, "Sighting Rekindles Manhunt," *Denver Post*, July 1, 1998; Electa Draper,

"Searchers Torch Riverbanks," *Denver Post*, July 3, 1998; Chuck Slothower, "Remains May Be '98 Cop-Killer Suspect, *Durango Herald*, June 6, 2007; Ben Winslow, "Manhunt: A 9-Year Mystery May Be Solved," *Deseret News*, June 7, 2007.

III. SNOWBOUND

Information on avalanche safety was obtained from the Internet online information page, "Avalanche Awareness," (*bsidc.org/snow/avalanche/*) maintained by the National Snow and Ice Data Center, University of Colorado, Boulder, on January 8, 2008.

Killed in Their Sleep–Mike Jenkins, "3 Skiers Buried and Killed," in Accidents, 1996–1997, www.avalanche.org.

A Warm-Weather Avalanche–AP, "Avalanche Kills Climber, Injures 5 Others," *Seattle Post-Intelligencer*, June 12, 1998; Farabee, *Death, Daring and Disaster*, pp. 450–451.

A Close Call–Andy Gleason, "Cabin Destroyed with Man Inside," in Accidents, 1997–1998, www.avalanche.org.

An "Urban" Avalanche and Its Wild Victims–Hans Ibold, "Avalanches Wreak Havoc in Hailey, Heagle Peak Damaged, Deer Herd Killed," *Idaho Mountain Express*, February 1999.

Snowdog–Garth Ferber, "1 Hungry Pooch," in Accidents, 1999–2000, www.avalanche.org.

IV. LOST HORIZON: AIR ACCIDENTS

For general information on flying conditions in the intermountain West: www.mountainflying.com.

Fallen Angel–Erin McCormick, and Eve Mitchell, "The Tragic Flight of Jessica Dubroff," *San Francisco Examiner*, April 14, 1996; AP, "Dubroff Policies at Issue in Judge Settling Dispute in Young Pilot's Death," *Denver Post*, December 21, 1997; Patricia Smith, "Good for Jessica—She Lived Her Dream," *Denver Post*, April 16, 1996; Maureen Dowd, "Jessica Dubroff: A Father's Quest for Celebrity Turns Deadly," *New York Times*, April 16, 1996; Catalina Ortiz,

"200 Mourners Bid Girl Pilot Farewell," *Denver Post*, April 16, 1996; National Transportation Safety Board Report SEA96MA079.

The Bermuda Triangle of the Rockies?–Chris Plante, "Air Force: Mysterious Jet Crash a Suicide," CNN.com, October 24, 1997; Jeffrey Leib, "Veteran Pilot Folds Wings," *Denver Post*, November 9, 2003; National Transportation Safety Board Report DCA01MA034; Jeffrey Leib, Michelle Flucher, Carlos Illescas, and Brent Gardner-Smith, "Aspen Air Crash Kills 18; Plane Misses Airport by Half a Mile," *Denver Post*, March 30, 2002; Nancy Lofholm, "Governor Stunned by Wreckage 'That Could Have Befallen Any of Us,'" *Denver Post*, March 31, 2001; Kevin Vaughan, M. E. Springelmeyer, and Deborah Frazier, "Doomed Jet Faced Deadline," *Rocky Mountain News*, March 31, 2001.

Firefall: Heroes in the Sky–Stephen J. Pyne, *Fire in America: A Cultural History of Wildland and Rural Fire* (Princeton, NJ: Princeton University Press, 1982), pp. 439, 440, 441–443; Dougles G. Gantenbein, *A Season of Fire: Four Months on the Firelines of America's Forests* (New York: Tarcher Penguin, 2003), pp. 182–184; Thomas McGarry, "Burns and Crashes," *www.govexec.com*, June 15, 2003; National Transportation Safety Board Report LAX02GA201; Ed Vogel and Sean Whaley, "Air Tanker Crash: Three Die Fighting Fires," *Las Vegas Review-Journal*, June 18, 2002; Elizabeth Aguilera, "Remembering the Victims: Stollak Had a Big Appetite for Life," *Denver Post*, July 21, 2002; Coleman Cornelius, "Slurry Pilot Knew Plane's Perils: Daughter Had Pleaded with Stollak to Quit Before Fatal Accident," *Denver Post*, July 24, 2002; National Transportation Safety Board Report DEN02GA074.

V. TROUBLED WATERS

Clear, Still, but Still Dangerous: Open Water (Freshwater) Accidents–National Park Service, The Morning Report, Glen Canyon National Recreation Area (NV/AZ), Drowning, July 7, 2001; National Park Service, The Morning Report, Lake Mead National Recreation Area (NV/AZ), Wind Storm Rescue, April 19, 2002; National Park Service, The Morning

Report, Lake Mead National Recreation Area (UT/AZ), June 17, 2004; Farabee, *Death, Daring, and Disaster*, pp. 444–445.

Whitewater Wildernesses: Paddling Accidents–Ron Watters, "Whitewater River Accident Analysis," in Rena Koesler, and Ron Watters, *Proceedings of the 1995 International Conference on Outdoor Recreation and Education* (Pocatello: Idaho State University Press, 1996); Farabee, *Death, Daring, and Disaster*, p. 428; National Park Service, Grand Teton National Park, brochure revised June 2006; Rich Tosches, "Snake River's Rage Turned Float Trip Tragic," *Denver Post*, June 23, 2006.

The Weather Underground–AP, "Reno Man Safe After Four Friends Die in Utah Cave," *Reno Gazette-Journal*, August 19, 2005; Bruce Rogers, and Pat Helton, "Bower Cave: A Journey from Private to Public Ownership," *The Western Cave Conservancy*, Spring, 2005; Sara Israelson, and Jeremy Twitchell, "4 Drown in Cave," *Deseret News*, August 19, 2005.

In Hot Water–Lee H. Whittlesey, *Death in Yellowstone: Accidents and Foolhardiness in the First National Park* (Boulder, CO: Roberts Rinehart Publishers, 1995), pp. 3–4; Michael Milstein, "Park Workers Leaped into Pool," *Billings Gazette*, August 24, 2000; *Buchi v. The United States of America*, United States District Court for the District of Wyoming, February 6, 2004.

VI. BIBLICAL RAINS

Gone in a Flash–AP, "Slot Canyon Tragedy Claims 11 Lives," August 13, 1997; Farabee, *Death, Daring, and Disaster*, pp. 446–447; Department of the Interior, U.S. Geological Survey, Fact Sheet 2006-3095; Carl Abbott, Stephen J. Leonard, and David McComb, *Colorado: A History of the Centennial State* (Boulder: Colorado Associated University Press, 1982), p. 310; Andra Coberly, "Just So Much Water," *Fort Collins Weekly*, July 28, 2007; Nolan J. Doesken, and Thomas B. McKee, "An Analysis of Rainfall for the July 28, 1997 Flood in Fort Collins, Colorado," Colorado Climate Center, Atmospheric Science Department, Colorado State University.

VII. The Sky Above, the Earth Below: More Severe Weather;
Climate Change, and the Future of Western Wildlands

For Colorado's winter of 2006-2007 and related weather phenomena:
"El Nino Gains Strength," *NOAA Magazine*, December 7, 2007;
Richard A. Keen, Skywatch West: *The Complete Weather Guide*
(Golden, CO: Fulcrum Publishing, 2004), p. xiv; Theodore Roosevelt, "Winter Weather, c. 1877," in *Eyewitness to the Old West:
Firsthand Accounts of Exploration, Adventure, and Peril*, edited by
Richard Scott (Lanham, MD: Roberts Rinehart Publishers, 2002, p.
371.

Serious Heat–Edward Abbey, *Desert Solitaire: A Season in the Wilderness* (New York, Touchstone, 1968), pp. 6, 10; Robert C. Balling,
and Sandra W. Brazel, "The Myth of Increasing Moisture Levels in
Phoenix," *Climate of Phoenix, Arizona*, online paper, Office of Climatology, Arizona State University, 1996; Farabee, *Death, Daring,
and Disaster*, p. 348; Steve Miller, "Familes of 11 Dead Illegals to
Sue U.S.," *Washington Times*, May 11, 2002; *Reynaldo Ambros-Marcial, et al. v. The United States*, United States District Court for
the District of Arizona, July 12, 2005; Pyne, *Fire in America*, p. 11;
Stephen J. Pyne, *Tending Fire: Coping with Wildland Fires* (Washington, DC: Island Press, 2004), p. 197; "Wildland Fire in Yellowstone," Yellowstone National Park website, National Park Service;
Sebastian Junger, "Blowup: What Went Wrong at Storm King Mountain," in *Fire*, pp. 51, 54; Bret W. Butler, Robert A. Bartlette, Larry
S. Bradshaw, Jack D. Cohen, Patricia L. Andrews, Ted Putnam, and
Richard J. Mangan, "Fire Behavior Associated with the 1994 South
Canyon Fire on Storm King Mountain, Colorado," Rocky Mountain Research Station, 1998.

Fire in the Sky–"Lightning Fatalities, Injuries, and Damage Reports in
the United States," www.lightningsafety.com, National Lightning Safety
Institute, August 27, 2007; Keen, *Skywatch West*, p. 59, 74–75;
American Meteorological Society, "Updated AMS Recommendations
for Lightning Safety—2002," NOAA website, August 27, 2007;
Vanessa Miller, "Boulder Man Hit by Lightning on Mount Elbert,"
Daily Camera, August 16, 2007.

Mighty Winds–Theodore T. Fujita, "The Teton-Yellowstone Tornado of 21 July 1987," *American Meteorological Society Monthly Weather Review*, September 1989; John Ritter, "Salt Lake Relieved Tornado Was Not Worse," *USA Today*, August 13, 1999; Keen, *Skywatch West*, p. 98; Bob Glancy, "Colorado Tornado Facts," *Colorado Climate*, Summer 2001; Dick Foster, Bill Scanlon, and Lisa Ryckman, "Holly Suffers Nature's Fury, Unpredictably," *Rocky Mountain News*, March 30, 2007; Emily Tienken, "Wind Leaves Damage and Power Outages," *Daily Camera*, June 8, 2007; Anthony L. Westerling, Daniel R. Cayan, Timothy J. Brown, Beth L. Hall, and Laurance G. Riddle, "Climate, Santa Ana Winds, and Autumn Wildfires in Southern California," *Eos Colume 85*, Number 31, August 3, 2004; Michael Stetz, and Chris Moran, "Witnesses Say 12 Who Died Had Little Chance," *San Diego Union-Tribune*, November 1, 2003. Raymond Chandler, "The Red Wind," in *The Black Lizard Big Book of Pulps* (New York: Vintage, 2007); Joan Didion, *Slouching Toward Bethlehem* (New York: Modern Library, 2000).

Winds of Change?–Kristi Marohn, "When It Comes to Global Warming, He's Got Something to Say," *St. Cloud Times* online edition, September 7, 2007; Brian Fagan, *The Long Summer: How Climate Changed Civilization* (New York: Basic Books, 2004), 217; S. T. Gray, L. J. Graumlich, and J. L. Betancourt, "Yellowstone National Park Precipitation Since AD 1173," *Quaternary Research* 68 (2007); Joe Verengia, "Geologists Unexpectedly Find 100 Glaciers in Colorado," *Hawaii Tribune Herald*, October 7, 2001; Stephen Saunders, and Tom Easley, *Losing Ground: Western National Parks Endangered by Climate Disruption* (New York: National Resources Defense Council, 2006) p. 10; CanWest News Service, "Climate Change Could Be Causing Cougar Attacks: Expert," *National Post*, August 29, 2007; "Steam Explosions, Earthquakes, and Volcanic Eruptions—What's in Yellowstone's Future?" U.S. Geological Survey Fact Sheet 2005–3024; National Parks and Conservation Association, "Gateways to Yellowstone: Protecting the Wild Heart of a Region's Thriving Economy," May 2006.

VIII. WILD STILL: TWO WEEKS IN SEPTEMBER

Miles Blumhardt, "Hikers Found Alive, Unharmed," *The Coloradoan*, September 7, 2007; Laurie-Claire Corson, "Cougar Kills Miniature Horse Near Nederland," *Daily Camera*; Vanessa Miller, "Bear-Proof Laws Mulled," *Daily Camera*, September 15, 2007; "Belgrade Man Describes Grizzly Bear Attack," *Great Falls Tribune*, September 15, 2007; Arthur H. Rotstein, "Migrant Deaths Rising in Arizona," *Daily Camera*, September 15, 2007; Tom Gardner, "Technology May Have Abandoned Its Longtime Friend Steve Fossett," SignonSandiego.com, September 21, 2007.